Roughing It Easy

Roughing
It Easy

DIAN THOMAS

THE DIAN THOMAS COMPANY
SALT LAKE CITY, UTAH

Roughing It Easy.
Copyright © 1994 by Dian Thomas. Printed and bound in the United States of America. All rights reserved. No part of this book may be reproduced in any form or by any electronic or mechanical means including information storage and retrieval systems without permission in writing from the publisher, except by a reviewer, who may quote brief passages in a review. Published by Dian Thomas Publishing Company, P.O. Box 171107, Holladay, UT 84117. Revised edition.

Distributed by Betterway Books, an imprint of F&W Publications, Inc., 1507 Dana Avenue, Cincinnati, OH 45207. 1-800-289-0963.

98 97 96 95   5 4 3 2

Library of Congress Cataloging in Publication Data

Thomas, Dian, 1945-
    Roughing it easy / by Dian Thomas — Rev. ed.
        p.   cm.
    Includes index.
    ISBN 0-9621257-3-3
    1. Outdoor cookery. 2. Camping. I. Title.
TX823.T49   1994
641.5'782 — dc20   94-9876
                                                                    CIP

Acknowledgments

A special thanks goes to Budge Wallis, who came to me in pursuit of a new book. It was his vision and foresight that sparked the possibility of a new edition. Thank you, Catherine Brohaugh, for combining all of my material into one packed volume of ideas. Bill Brohaugh, Lynn Perrigo, Diane King, Julie Nichols, Deanna DeLong, Mike Tuskes and Sandy Conopeotis assisted in developing this project into a new volume. I'm very grateful to my parents, who introduced me to outdoor living.

Environmental Awareness

Brighton Camp, which is nestled in the Wasatch Mountains, gave me the opportunity to explore and experience nature in its majestic surroundings. I've had wonderful experiences camping and enjoying the out-of-doors throughout my life.

With the hopes that future generations will be able to enjoy outdoor experiences like I have, I would like to pass along some thoughts on how to be kinder to our environment. Low impact camping is the key to providing outdoor opportunities for future generations. With more people enjoying the outdoors, the impact on nature is increased, which requires us to be more responsible. Forty years ago, there were no fire rings in campgrounds so we made our own with rocks. Backpacking stoves were nonexistent and camping groups often cut branches to sleep on at night. Today, for the sake of the environment, we've had to change our philosophy of camping to a less destructive one.

It is my hope that as you use the *roughing it easy* ideas contained in this book, you will be increasingly sensitive to your impact on the out-of-doors.

Preface

Camping appeals to the pioneer in all of us. Whether to introduce your kids to the solace of a quiet wooded space or to bolster a sense of independence and self-sustenance, camping provides a much needed breather in our ever more hectic daily lives. It is my hope that *Roughing It Easy* will help you and your family enjoy the companionship and camaraderie an outdoor camping experience can provide. This book will ease you into camping if you've never done it before, and will give helpful tips to the experienced camper to make your outings go more smoothly.

Camping provides the opportunity for enormous creativity. (Imagine how creative pioneers had to be.) When released from the constraints of daily conveniences, you will surprise yourself with the many fun and creative ways you handle the everyday necessities of life. For instance, think you can't bake a cake on an overnight camping trip? You can. Cooking in an outdoor kitchen demands some particular skills campers can develop with a few basic facts and guidelines. Even the most inexperienced cook can turn out a delicious outdoor meal or organize an entire camping trip.

Planning is the key to a successful camping trip. This book provides guidelines for destination selection, trip length and clothing needs. You will learn how to set up an outdoor home away from home, how to plan and shop for a complete menu, and how to cook foods using many different methods. Charts for menu planning, shopping trips, cooking methods and budgeting time are some of the most helpful items in the book. You will also be interested in the substitute list—what foods can be substituted for other items in an emergency.

Hints that help make camping easier appear in every section. For example, soaping pans on the outside before putting them on the heat will keep them from blackening. Baking an individual cake inside an orange peel wrapped in foil not only saves dishes but adds a delicate orange flavor to the cake. You will learn how to start fires without matches by using batteries and steel wool or a bow drill, and you will learn how to cook two separate dishes in a Dutch oven using aluminum foil dividers. I've included tested recipes and methods of cooking, along with clear instructions and illustrations that will help make your camping fun. And, after you master these skills, you can use the principles outlined to help you create ideas of your own.

From a backyard barbecue to winter camping adventures, I hope this book helps you and your family Rough It Easy!

CHAPTER 1

Taking the First Steps Outdoors

I f you want to get a taste of camping *before* actually camping, your family room (not to mention your backyard) is a great place to experiment. Or, perhaps, in the dead of winter, you itch for the one-of-a-kind taste of a fire-cooked meal. This chapter will give you a taste of the great outdoors — just beyond your kitchen door.

Cooking in Your Fireplace

You don't have to stand out in the cold to barbecue during winter. Use your fireplace — after all, this is how people cooked before there were ovens (Figure 1-1). First, get a good steady fire going in the center of the fireplace. Let the fire burn down to enough coals for cooking (this will take 30 to 40 minutes). Hardwoods provide the best coals for cooking in your fireplace. Build up the fire on one side of the fireplace and pull the coals over to

Figure 1-1. Learning how to cook using your fireplace

the other side to cook on. Put down four bricks—two stacked on top of each other and placed on the side of the fireplace you plan to cook on. As the coals begin to burn down, use a small shovel to place the coals between the two stacks of bricks. You may place foil-wrapped items directly on the coals or place a rack on the bricks and then cook on it. To raise the temperature, remove two bricks or add more coals under the rack. To lower the temperature, add more bricks or remove coals from under the rack.

For baking, you'll need to use a Dutch oven. It's also fun to use a stick for cooking hot dogs or marshmallows. And, if you plan to cook a lot in the fireplace, cover the hearth with aluminum foil. During times of emergency, such as power outages, your skills in using the fireplace will add to your ability to survive in comfort.

ENCHILADA PIE—A SUPER SUPPER

Method: *Dutch oven*
Time: *30 minutes*

- Working over an open fire, brown

  1 medium onion, chopped
  ½ teaspoon salt
  2 pounds ground beef

- Drain off drippings and add

  1 10¾-ounce can condensed
      tomato soup
  2 10-ounce cans mild
      enchilada sauce
  1 cup water

- Simmer 5 minutes. Spoon ¼ of mixture into a medium bowl.
- Arrange over mixture remaining in pan
- Alternate in 3 layers

  2 to 3 8-inch flour tortillas
  meat mixture
  2 cups (8 ounces) shredded
      cheddar or mozzarella
      cheese
  tortillas

Replace lid on Dutch oven. Simmer 7 to 10 minutes or until cheese melts and tortillas soften. Serve pie with remaining tortillas as side bread. Serves 6 to 8 (Figure 1-2).

Figure 1-2. Enchilada pie

MEAT LOAF IN AN ONION—AN UNUSUAL FAMILY TREAT

Method: *Foil cooking*

Time: *40 minutes*

- Cut and set aside

  3 12 × 14-inch rectangles of heavy-duty foil

- In a medium bowl, mix

  1 pound lean ground beef
  1 egg
  ⅛ teaspoon pepper
  ½ teaspoon salt
  ½ teaspoon dry mustard

- Cut in half horizontally and remove centers, leaving ½-inch shell of

  3 medium onions

- Chop onion centers.

- Stir

  2 tablespoons onion into meat mixture

- Spoon

  meat mixture into 3 onion halves, rounding on top

Place remaining onion halves on top of filled onion halves. Place one filled onion on each piece of foil. Bring ends of foil up over onion. Fold foil down in small folds. Press sides of foil close to onion. Flatten ends and roll toward onion. Cook on coals 15 minutes on each side. Serves 3 (Figure 1-3).

Figure 1-3.
Meat loaf in an
onion

Figure 1-4. Banana boat

Roughing It Easy

BANANA BOAT—A DELICIOUS DESSERT TO COOK IN COALS

Method: *Foil cooking*

Time: *10 minutes*

- With knife starting at stem ends, cut through top peel from one end to the other of   4 bananas
- Spread bananas apart and fill with   ½ cup milk chocolate chips

                                           ½ cup miniature marshmallows

Wrap securely in heavy-duty foil. Heat 5 minutes over coals until chocolate and marshmallows melt. Serves 4 (Figure 1-4).

Camping in Your Own Backyard

Cooking a family meal in the fireplace is an exciting change for a dreary winter evening, but once the jonquil buds start poking their yellow caps through the ground, everyone is eager for an outing. These tips will make a backyard barbecue or a weekend camping trip more fun for all. (For the discussion on starting charcoal briquets, see pages 64-66.)

Improvised Barbecues

You can make an improvised barbecue with a metal garbage can lid, three bricks and some dirt, sand or gravel.

On a flat area free of grass, leaves or other debris, place three bricks so they will support a garbage can lid turned upside down. (Figure 1-5.) Place a metal lid upside down on the bricks and fill the lid with dirt, sand or gravel. The dirt will act as insulation to protect the lid. Cover with aluminum foil and then put the charcoal briquets on top of the aluminum foil and light. This is excellent for a hot dog roast or for foil dinners.

When you are through, simply pour the dirt out of the lid and the lid is still reusable on your garbage can.

Child's Wagon Barbecue

Wheel a child's wagon where it will be most convenient for cooking. If you plan to leave the dirt in the wagon for a long period of time, be sure the wagon is painted, and then cover the wagon with foil to keep the moisture from causing the wagon to rust. (Figure 1-6.) Fill the wagon with sand, dirt or gravel. Then place

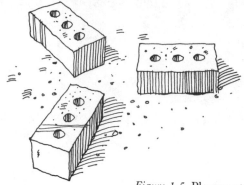

Figure 1-5. Placement of the bricks for an improvised barbecue

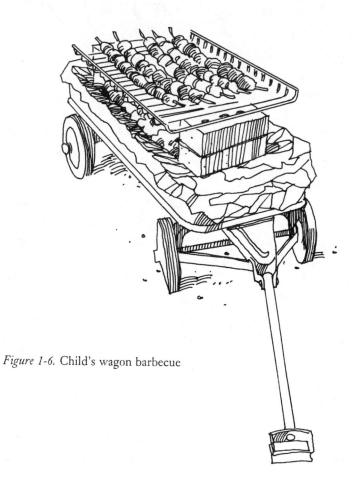

Figure 1-6. Child's wagon barbecue

foil over the sand, dirt or gravel so the coals do not nest into the dirt and cut off the air circulation necessary for proper burning. Place the charcoal briquets on the foil and light as directed on the package. For foil or stick cooking (discussed in chapters seven and nine), you are ready to cook. This is a great way for children to enjoy cooking a hot dog or roasting marshmallows. For grilling, place a brick on both sides of the wagon and set a rack across the bricks. (A word of caution: Do not use a refrigerator rack; some contain a harmful substance that is released by the heat.)

Wheelbarrow Grill

You can make a versatile barbecue that will handle a whole meal by using a wheelbarrow, a few bricks, some foil and dirt. (Figure 1-7.) The great advantage of this grill is that it can be wheeled wherever you want and is just the right height for you to sit on a lawn chair and roast marshmallows, hot dogs or even apples. The wheelbarrow provides enough space for a rotisserie and grill, as well as cooking directly on the coals.

To set up a wheelbarrow grill, fill the wheelbarrow with gravel, sand or dirt until it is about 6 inches deep, which should insulate the wheelbarrow from the heat. For efficient briquet cooking, cover the area where the briquets will be placed with

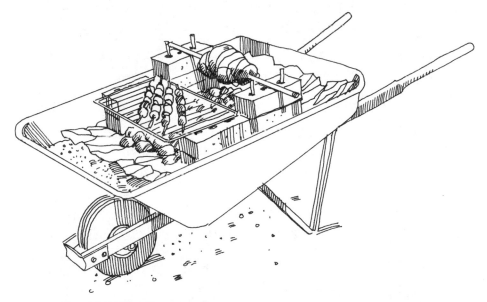

Figure 1-7. Wheelbarrow grill

extra-heavy aluminum foil. Stack the briquets in the center of the wheelbarrow and light them. When they are hot, spread them over the foil.

Once the briquets are burning, line the sides of the wheelbarrow with bricks, then place a large grill across them for barbecuing flat pieces of meat. (For easy cleaning, spray the rack with nonstick cooking spray before using.) You can regulate the cooking temperature by adding or taking away bricks to raise or lower your grill. Increase the heat by using fewer bricks, decrease it by adding more. The most efficient grill height is 3 to 5 inches above the coals. If you simply want to use the coals for stick cooking, you don't need to bother with the bricks or rack.

You can also try one of the following arrangements:

- **Rotisserie, grill and open coals.** Use bricks on the back for a rotisserie, bricks just in front to support a wire rack, and then leave an open space for cooking over coals.
- **Rotisserie and open grill.** Stack bricks at the back for a rotisserie and bricks along the side with a rack on top of them for a grill.
- **Grill.** Place bricks in the four corners and put a rack on top.
- **Open coals.** Cook directly on or over the coals using the foil or stick cooking methods.

You may want to slide a pair of mitt-type pot holders onto the handles of the wheelbarrow so they will be handy while you are grilling. When you are done using the grill and the briquets have cooled, cover the wheelbarrow so the dirt doesn't get wet from rain or dew. (Moisture will cause the bottom of the wheelbarrow to rust.) If you keep it covered with heavy plastic when not in use, one load of dirt should last the entire summer.

Backyard Conveniences

There never seems to be enough room for all the goodies offered in a backyard barbecue — flat, stable spaces for serving especially seem to be at a premium. Here are a couple of tips for making your barbecue go more smoothly for you and your guests.

Ironing Board Buffet

Change your ironing board into a portable serving table. Keep it from tipping by placing sandbags over the bar or putting bricks against the legs. Cover it with a plastic cover and then a decorative tablecloth. Arrange plates, cups and flatware so people can pick them up as they go through the buffet line.

Laundry Basket Ice Chest

Line a small laundry basket with a heavy-duty garbage bag or plastic. Fill the basket with crushed ice and place pop cans and bottles down in the ice to keep cool. If the basket is too large, fill the bottom half with crushed newspaper, then place the plastic bag or garbage bag on top of the newspaper.

Wheelbarrow Party-Server

Line a wheelbarrow with plastic (optional) and fill it with ice — it's ideal for serving salads and canned pop. The wheelbarrow can be rolled to a convenient, shady spot for serving. The ice will keep drinks and salads cool.

Insect-Proofing Your Food

Using embroidery hoops, stretch plastic wrap across the smaller hoop, place the larger hoop over the smaller one and secure the hoops in place. Use this as a cover over salads or other food. It is great to use for protecting food from insects while still allowing your guests to see what's inside.

Another way to keep insects off of your food is to use two electric fans, one on each side of the picnic table. However, be sure to keep your plates and cups weighted down with food and liquid so they don't fly away too!

MAKE ICE CREAM WITH YOUR FEET!

Nothing tops off a summer evening like homemade ice cream! This recipe is quick and easy, and your kids will want to help.

KICK-THE-CAN ICE CREAM

- In a   1 pound coffee can
- Combine   ¾ cup whole milk

                                  1 cup cream

                                  ⅓ cup sugar

                                  ½ teaspoon vanilla

                                  any flavoring (chocolate syrup, raspberry, etc.)

- Place plastic lid on 1 pound can and put into   3 pound coffee can
- Pack with   crushed ice

                                  ¾ cup salt or rock salt

Put a plastic lid on the 3-pound coffee can. Roll the can back and forth to a friend for 10 minutes. After 10 minutes of rolling, take the lid off and, with a table knife, scrape the ice cream off sides and stir into mixture. If it needs more freezing, drain water out of the large can. Place the small can back into the large can, pack with ice and salt or rock salt, and roll 5 minutes more.

Roughing It Easy

CHAPTER 2

Planning

The first ingredient of successful camping is a good plan. Consider the time, destination, activities, food, personal equipment and organizing of group tasks. This chapter is designed to give you basic information and helpful ideas on all those things you need to do before pitching camp. Use it to help make your preliminary trip decisions.

Time

All the other preplanning for a trip, of course, depends on the amount of time you have. Will the trip be just for the morning or afternoon? Will it be for overnight, for a weekend or longer? Backpacking trips and long camping trips will take more careful planning than an evening cookout. You may even need to plan far enough in advance to obtain a permit or make a reservation.

Destination

Your destination will determine how carefully you plan the trip. As much pertinent information as possible should be gathered about the selected destination so that accurate planning and preparation can be made. Considerations of climate and length of trip dictate the amount and type of clothing to take. You should make careful purchases for locations where shopping is impossible. Drinking water may have to be transported to areas where no water is available.

Activities

It is important that you organize each day's activities, then plan the equipment, clothing and meals around them. A long afternoon hike, for example, will allow just enough time for a one-pot meal to simmer on the coals. For an all-day hike, on the other hand, plan a hearty breakfast, a simple sack lunch carried in a day pack or sack around the belt, and a snack for energy; if you intend to return to camp late, plan a meal that is quick to prepare or was left to cook while you were away.

Group Organization Plan

A detailed plan to involve all the camping participants will make your experience more satisfying for everyone. This plan will vary depending on the numbers and ages of those in the group and the activities already planned. For example, if your first meal at camp has already been cooked, this will give campers more time to unpack and get settled. If campers are involved beforehand in organizing the trip, if they know exactly what needs to be done, and if each of them has chosen a particular assignment for which he or she will be responsible, everything should run smoothly. Children as well as adults will gain more from the camping experience if they share responsibilities. The following ideas may help in making work assignments.

Trip Responsibilities for Group Camping

Everyone should help in some area of the total camping operation. If the campout involves more than a few close friends or family members, consider these possible designated roles:

- **Group leader:** Choose a group leader who will coordinate all activities and responsibilities.
- **First-aid assistant:** The camp "doctor" or "nurse" arranges first-aid supplies and cares for minor first-aid problems.
- **Equipment specialist:** This person packs the camping equipment, sees that it is properly cared for at camp, and returns each piece to its proper place.
- **Shopping specialist:** Although everyone should help plan and shop for meals, one person should compile the shopping list and organize the shopping.
- **Photographer:** A person especially talented in taking pictures should keep a photographic record of activities.
- **Journalist:** A camp record will be a valuable keepsake for everyone.
- **Conservation specialist:** One person should take the responsi-

bility of seeing that the group sets up conservation standards and keeps them.

- **Fire specialist:** Someone should make sure that all fires are built according to proper safety standards and that they are tended and properly extinguished.
- **Games specialist:** One person should be in charge of planning, organizing and gathering equipment for games.
- **Song leader:** Sometimes one person should act as song leader although everyone will join in singing and choosing songs.
- **Campsite assistant:** This person should help the group leader to direct the camp set up and cleanup.
- **Crafts director:** A person who enjoys creating craft projects and organizing supplies and materials should be selected for this position.
- **Hike director:** This person acquires maps of the area, checks people in and out of the camping area and organizes hikes.
- **Kitchen specialist:** Acting as chef, this person should direct the various campers as each group participates in meal preparation and cleanup.

Meal Responsibility

As well as participating in general camp responsibilities, each camper should join in some aspect of meal preparation and cleanup. The following system works very well with a group of six or more who plan to cook at least three meals. Divide the campers into three small groups. Each group will have one of the following duties: (1) fire building, (2) cooking and (3) cleaning up. The groups will switch duties at each meal until everyone has had the opportunity to be a fire builder, a cook and a cleanup person.

Fire Builders

- Gather and cut plenty of wood for the fire. Some parks and national forests restrict wood gathering, so first check to see if it is permitted. If firewood is not available, take plenty from home.
- Have a shovel and bucket of water on hand in case the fire gets out of control.
- Consult the cooks and build the type of fire they request early enough to allow for ample coals if they are required.

- Keep the fire burning and assign someone to care for it as long as it burns.
- Extinguish the fire.

Cooks
- Tell the fire builders which type of fire is needed and when to start it.
- Plan carefully how much time will be required to cook each item and when its preparation should begin.
- Organize and set up the kitchen.
- Soap the outsides of all kettles to be used in the open fire.
- Prepare and cook all food.

Cleanup
- Prepare a centerpiece and set the table.
- Make sure garbage areas are established.
- Check to see that all food is properly stored.
- When there is room on the fire — hopefully this will be at least twenty minutes or more before it is time to wash the dishes — put the dishwater on to heat.
- Prepare the area for dishwashing.
- Put leftover food away.
- Wash all dishes and cooking utensils.
- Make sure that everything in the camp is put away and the camp area is cleaned.

Included on the next three pages is a master planning chart that will help you carry out the above suggestions.

MASTER PLANNING CHART

Trip Planning Leader(s):

_____

_____

_____

Decisions:

Time of stay _____

Dates of trip _____

Destination _____

Persons Going on Trip:

_____

_____

_____

_____

Be Sure to Check:

Things to Consider	Person in Charge	Completed
Trip Costs		
Reservations		
Type of transportation		
Route of travel (map)		
Insurance		
Other		

Planning Chairperson (fill out own chart below):

Chairperson	Name	Responsibilities
Activities		Plan all activities for trip.
Menus		Check activities; plan all menus around activities.
Equipment		Plan all equipment needs, where to get them, what will be needed.
Meal duties		Organize everybody into small groups to prepare meals and clean up.
Group tasks		Give the entire group specific camp duties.

Chart for Activities Chairperson:

Days	Morning	Afternoon	Evening
1			
2			
3			

Chart for Menus Chairperson; see chapter six:

Chart for Equipment Chairperson:

Kinds of Equipment	Packer	Put Away
Basic camping equipment (see list in chapter three)		
Kitchen equipment (see list in chapter three)		
Games — sports		
Arts and crafts		

Chart for Meal Duties Chairperson:

Days	Meal	Fire Builders	Cooks	Cleanup
	Breakfast			
1	Lunch			
	Dinner			
	Breakfast			
2	Lunch			
	Dinner			
	Breakfast			
3	Lunch			
	Dinner			

Chart for Group Tasks Chairperson

Duty	Name	Responsibilities
Group leader		Coordinate all activities, responsibilities.
Shopping specialist		Receive menus; compile lists for shopping.
Equipment specialist		Pack, care for, and put away all needed equipment.
Campsite assistant		Help group leader direct setup and cleanup.
Kitchen specialist		Direct groups in meal preparation and cleanup.
Fire specialist		Check fire area; help fire builders in building, tending, extinguishing.
First-aid assistant		Order supplies and give list to shopping specialist; care for minor problems.
Conservation specialist		Help group set up standards and keep them at camp.
Activities coordinator		Keep all people aware of pending activities and help with each one.
Games specialist		Direct all planned games at camp.
Hike director		Direct all hikes at camp.
Crafts director		Direct all crafts at camp.
Song leader		Lead the singing while at camp; take charge of choosing songs to sing.
Journalist		Record camp happenings; make a copy for all campers.
Photographer		Bring camera and film; take pictures; take charge of getting film developed.

CHAPTER 3

Equipment

Equipment for any kind of outdoor activity comes in so many shapes and sizes that, if you are like most people, you could never collect — or afford — all those "just right" and expensive trappings. You would need a fortune to buy them, a transportation fleet to carry them, and a computer system to keep everything cataloged and organized.

On the other hand, if you devise your own traveling and camping equipment, you'll be able to have all the gear you'll ever need, without great expense. Many useful items can be made or improvised from household articles. You will be surprised at what you can turn out with a few basic tools and a little know-how. Although the results may not qualify for a "Most Beautiful Campsite" award, the equipment will be functional, and that is the most important requirement.

The goal of this chapter is to help you experience the thrill that can come from creating your own equipment and adapting it to your personal uses.

General Camping Equipment

Consider the safety and accessibility of the camping area and the length of your stay before you plan what equipment to take. An area you drive to will allow more pieces of equipment than one you hike into. An afternoon cookout will require less equipment than a week's stay. For trips that last overnight or longer, tarps, ground cloths or ponchos are handy. They can be placed under sleeping equipment, used to cover wood piles (especially when it rains), or used as a shelter if needed.

When considering equipment, remember to take as little as possible and to take equipment that can be used in many different ways.

Fire Equipment

A shovel and some kind of water bucket are very important if open fires are planned. Keep them close to the fire in case the fire spreads. A saw can be faster for cutting wood than an ax, especially for those who are not skilled in using an ax.

Another important item of equipment to consider is a pair of heat-proof gloves. They are helpful for setting pans on and removing them from the fire, for removing coals or aluminum packages, and for clearing the coals off the top of a Dutch oven as well as for removing its lid. Use them in any way you would use a hot pad. If heat-proof gloves are impossible to purchase, use leather or other heavy gloves.

Personal Equipment

It's hard to escape housekeeping and personal grooming concerns, especially while camping or traveling, but you can make these easy and fun if you set your creative talents free to work for you. All you need are a few ideas to help you get started. Here are some starting points to spark your imagination.

Clothing

Plan clothing to give protection and warmth while allowing freedom for activities. Take only the essentials.

1. *Shoes.* Shoes are especially important if you plan to hike. Choose a sturdy, comfortable pair that provide support and protection. Avoid tennis shoes since they give neither. Break in new shoes at home first. Otherwise, you'll spend your trip soaking blistered feet.
2. *Socks.* Lightweight socks are good to wear around camp, but for hiking, wool socks are best because they absorb moisture and cushion the feet. Wearing two pairs of socks during a hike—a light pair under a heavier pair—will help prevent blister-causing friction. Carry Band-Aids or moleskin and tape them over areas rubbed by your shoes before these areas have a chance to blister.
3. *Pants.* Long, sturdy pants will provide protection from branches, sharp rocks, sunburn, fire or hot cooking grease. Tight-fitting pants restrain freedom and should be avoided.

4. *Shirts.* Long sleeves provide the best protection against sunburn, insects and evening coolness.
5. *Hat.* A hat will give some protection against the sun and will hold in body heat during cool weather.
6. *Jacket.* A water-repellent jacket is best, but either a large plastic bag or a square of plastic can be used as an improvised poncho. Plastic is lightweight and easy to carry. To turn a large plastic bag into a rain cover, turn the bag upside down. Cut a hole at the bottom of the bag for your head, and then cut holes on both sides of the bag for your arms. This is great to take on hikes for that unexpected cloud burst.
7. *Coat.* A warm coat is a welcome relief from night and early morning chill in some areas.

Cooking Equipment

The best way to decide what cooking equipment is needed is to plan menus, then make an itemized equipment list.

Take some basic utensils, at least one good pan or a Dutch oven, and a grill. You can improvise other pieces of equipment as needed from tin cans, plastic containers, aluminum foil and sticks. These items are helpful in many ways as utensils and can often be discarded at the end of the trip. (See chapter twelve for more on cooking equipment for backpackers.) Suggestions for improvising cooking equipment are as follows:

- Use a can for a rolling pin.
- Use a can to cut out hamburgers, biscuits or cookies. Punch a hole in the bottom of the empty can so that air can pass through.
- If you use a can for both cooking and serving food, there are fewer things to clean up.
- A #10 can may serve as a dishpan.
- If large enough, warm vegetables in the cans they come in to save utensils.
- Use heavy-duty foil to make a shallow pan into a deep pan. Place a large piece of foil in a cake pan. Press the foil into the bottom of the pan and bring it up the sides, extending the foil beyond the top of the pan (Figure 3-1). Decide approximately how deep you want the pan to be, then leave enough foil

Figure 3-1. Pan deepened with foil

Figure 3-2. Aluminum foil serving bowl

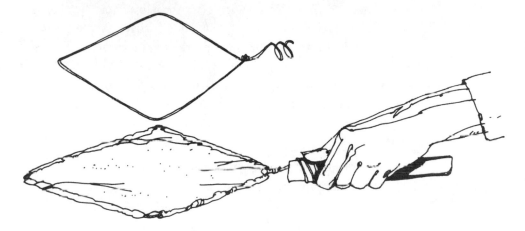

Figure 3-3. Foil-wire frying pan

extended above the top of the pan to achieve that depth. Finally, turn down the excess foil to make the sides stronger.

- Use aluminum foil shaped like a bowl for serving foods (Figure 3-2).
- Roll the edges of a piece of foil around a square made from a wire coat hanger to make a frying pan (Figure 3-3).
- Use heavy, self-sealing plastic bags for mixing foods.
- Use a clean stick as a stirring spoon.
- Cut out the sides and bottom of a plastic bleach bottle and use as a scoop.
- Line a #10 can with a gallon-sized, self-sealing bag and use

it as a serving container. When you are through, seal the top of the bag and place it in the cooler.

Other kitchen and cooking equipment to bring along includes:

- A plastic bottle with a pop-up top, useful for storing and using cooking oil. Fill the clean bottle with salad or cooking oil and label it "Cooking Oil." Keep the top down until you are ready to use the oil. If you're worried the top will pop up during travel, causing leaks, tape the top down.
- A Frisbee plate nester. On picnic and car trips, campers often use paper plates. The inexpensive kind does not hold its shape well unless it is reinforced by an additional plate or a "nester." A Frisbee, often taken along on camping trips for fun, is just the right shape to fit under a paper plate to help it hold its shape. You can even put a stack of plates in a frisbee. As you use the plates, just keep peeling them off the top of the stack. This is a great way to store your extra plates. Be sure to take your paper plates along when you buy the frisbee to be sure you purchase one big enough to hold a large stack of plates. As you can see, it may pay to invest in a few more Frisbees!

COOKING OUT WHILE CAMPING OUT

Whether your camping trip is for a week or just an overnighter, here are a few creative ways to put more fun into camping.

- A small tackle box placed near the grill can hold spatulas, knives and peelers in the bottom and seasonings in the trays. Look for a tackle box that will fit your needs.
- Fill a carpenter's apron with cooking necessities, such as a hot pad mitt, spatula, tongs and spices. Stitch the pockets to fit the utensils.

Shelter and Sleeping Bags

The selection and types of camping shelters on the market today are limitless. They range from tarps or sheets of plastic to multi-compartmental tents. In this chapter, you'll learn about the characteristics of good shelter, tent accessories, selecting a site for shelter, pitching and staking a tent, care of the shelter and the

varieties of sleeping bags available. There is additional information about shelter and sleeping bags in chapter twelve specifically
for lightweight camping.

Characteristics of Good Shelter

Sufficient Capacity

How many people will need to be sheltered at your camp? One,
three, six? How many little ones, big ones? How much equipment
will have to be stored, along with all the people, in case of rain?

If the tents are to be transported by car, you can afford to
take ones that are large and comfortable, with ample room for
several people to stand up. If you choose any of the following
styles, you should be assured of plenty of room for family living:
umbrella (Figure 3-4), cabin (Figure 3-5) and multicompartmental (Figure 3-6).

Weight and Bulk

Tents used in car camping can be heavier and bulkier than lightweight tents because it is not necessary to conserve weight or
space. A tent and poles may weigh up to 35 pounds or more.

Materials and Construction

Most tents are constructed from nylon or polyester. Nylon is
the most popular fabric because of its light weight and durability.
It is used in about 90 percent of the tents on the market. Occasionally big cabin tents are made from polyester. The polyester
resists fading and weather wear when exposed to the elements
over long periods of time.

The floor material is usually made from a urethane-coated
nylon and the sidewalls are generally made from nylon. The
roof will either be a coated nylon or have a separate coated nylon
rain-fly.

The stress points of a tent should be reinforced with a double
seam and the corners reinforced with an extra layer of fabric.
The seams should run in the direction of the support, which is
usually vertical, not horizontal. There is usually a horizontal
seam somewhere above the floor of the tent where the sidewalls
attach. This is to prevent water from coming through the seams
onto the floor. The tent poles are mostly made from lightweight
aluminum and the stakes are made from aluminum or plastic.

Figure 3-4. Umbrella tent. Better headroom than the tepee tent, but sloping walls limit the efficient use of floor space.

Figure 3-5. Cabin tent (wall tent). Basic *A* structure plus vertical walls. One disadvantage is that the guy ropes require time and effort to set up.

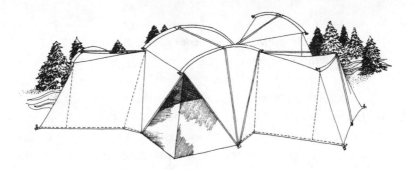

Figure 3-6. Multicompartmental tent. Different components combine into various tenting and shelter arrangements: kitchens, bedrooms, living rooms.

Ease of Assembly

Setting up a large tent often requires two or more people working together. Even if the tent is big with several poles for support, most modern tent designs make the task of assembly remarkably simple.

If you are assembling a tent for the first time, it is a good idea to do a dry run in your backyard. This will allow you to work out any problems and make sure you have all of the tent poles and pegs.

Tent Accessories

To be caught without necessary equipment when you are attempting to erect a tent is a sure-fire guarantee of a frustrating experience. Give a little forethought to each piece of equipment to avoid disasters at your campsite.

Stakes

Extra stakes are always handy. Since cabin tents tend to be like box kites when the wind blows, you might need extra metal stakes to secure your tent when the wind blows. If you find yourself in a sandy spot, strong plastic stakes with I beams hold well. If the ground is too soft to stake, guy lines can be tied to logs or rocks. They can also be buried in the ground for better security on a sandy beach.

Poles

All poles are made from aluminum and are strong and lightweight. They are also easy to replace should you lose one or irreparably bend one.

Guy Lines

Some tents may be rigged with guy lines for extra support and stabilization. Tents do not require guy lines except during a heavy wind.

Sleeping Bags

In car camping, as well as in all camping activities, a good sleeping bag ensures a good night's sleep so you can enjoy the next day's activities. The types of sleeping bags available vary from a blanket used in the hot desert to a down- or fiber-filled bag used in the cold. Discussed in this chapter are the heavier, synthetic-filled bags, which are best transported by automobiles. Later, in chapter twelve, bags to be used in lightweight camping are described.

Cuts of Bags

The rectangular bag is just that—a bag the same size at the bottom as at the top. The zipper on this bag zips across the bottom and up the side, allowing the bag to be opened out. It can be used as a quilt at times, or it can be zipped to another bag to be used as a double bag as long as the zippers match. A rectangular bag has space for moving your legs, providing greater comfort.

One disadvantage of the rectangular bag is that its greater space requires more body energy to warm it on cold nights.

The modified rectangular bag is similar to the rectangular, except that it tapers in toward the bottom, cutting down on the weight and the space required to transport it. It restricts movement in the feet area a little more than does the rectangular bag.

Sleeping Bag Construction

Shells for sleeping bags range from light canvas tops with flannel lining to synthetic materials for both top and lining. Most family camping bags are filled with synthetic fibers. The price for these synthetics varies with the performance of the bag and with the type of fill. Bags are generally filled with Hollofil® polyester, which varies in its thickness and compressability. Insulated sleeping pads are also available to place under sleeping bags for additional warmth and comfort. Hollofil does not absorb water, so when wet, sleeping bags dry quickly and are usually machine washable. For storage, it's best to keep your sleeping bags in oversized cotton stuff sacks or hung from rafters.

INNOVATIVE PILLOW IDEAS

- A quick pillow can be made by blowing up a large gallon-sized self-sealing plastic bag to the desired size and placing a shirt or slipcover over it.
- Another pillow can be made by folding your parka and placing it in a stuff sack. When your head is cold and you don't have a head section to your sleeping bag, place your head in the upper sleeve area of your parka and use it as a cap. A stocking cap or hooded sweatshirt also works well.

Pitching and Staking

If you learn to pitch your tent successfully, at least half the battle of trying to enjoy the out-of-doors will be won. The following suggestions might be of help.

Site Selection

Select a level spot and remove rocks and twigs. If no level spot is available, pitch the tent so that your head is uphill.

It is no longer advisable to dig a trench around your tent. Join the cause of the environmentalists and refrain from doing this. If possible, pitch your tent on high ground so that water runs away from it instead of into it. Avoid pitching your tent under a tree to be clear of falling branches. Remember, always leave the area better than you found it.

To prevent neck and shoulder sunburn when hiking, take a cap (baseball-type works very well), a piece of material and some Velcro®. You will need two measurements: the distance from the cap edge to just below the shoulder area plus 2 to 3 inches, and the distance around the back of the cap (be sure to allow for any stretch or cap adjustment). Cut a square of fabric to these measurements. Narrowly hem all edges, then sew one side of the Velcro to the top edge. Sew the other side of the Velcro to the outer cap edge. Stick them together whenever protection is needed.

The weather can change quickly when you're hiking or camping. Some nylon webbing and a sewing machine will ensure that each child has his or her jacket at all times. Measure the diagonal distance from the center back neck edge of the jacket to the side seam just below the arm hole and add 3 inches. Cut two pieces of webbing to this measurement. Sew the ends at the neck and side below the sleeve seam. Slip your child's arms through the webbing and he or she can wear the jacket just like a backpack.

Practice Pitching Your Tent

If your tent is new and you don't know how to pitch it, practice before you leave home. It is far easier to practice pitching your tent in familiar surroundings than on a dark, stormy night.

Tent Care

When you have chosen the type of shelter best for you and spent your hard-earned cash for it, you will expect it to serve you well. Remember—if you treat it well, it will reciprocate.

Keep It Dry

Be aware that nylon mildews if it remains wet. While you are breaking camp, let the sun dry your tent thoroughly. If you can't take the time, roll it up and stow it, but unfold it and dry it out at home. Then store it in a dry place. Stow your tent in its carrying case off of the floor so that it is not exposed to condensation or moisture.

Protect It From Puncture

We have mentioned that before you pitch your tent, you should remove rocks and twigs from the area where you will set it up. This protects your investment from puncture damage. Be wary of pitching the tent under a tree because falling branches can damage it as well. After the tent is pitched, keep rocks and sharp objects away from it. Punctures will turn into rips, and soon you will need a new tent. When you pack your tent, place the stakes and poles in separate stuff sacks to avoid damage to the tent.

Keep It Clean

To prolong the use of your tent, get into the habit of keeping the inside and outside clean. A ground cloth made of either coated nylon or plastic that is 6 millimeters or thicker will keep grime and dirt off the bottom of the tent. A nylon whisk broom can keep the twigs and dirt brushed out. You'll find it worth the extra time it takes to keep the floor of your shelter clean.

General Camping Equipment

The following is a checklist of general camping equipment, cooking equipment and utensils, kitchen supplies and other miscellaneous equipment you can use as a guide for a trip.

- ☐ Axe/hatchet/saw
- ☐ Batteries (for flashlight)
- ☐ Bucket
- ☐ Bulbs (for flashlight)
- ☐ Canteen
- ☐ Clothesline and clothespins
- ☐ Compass
- ☐ Flashlight
- ☐ Lantern (extra mantles and fuel)
- ☐ Lashing twine
- ☐ Maps
- ☐ Packs
- ☐ Rope (rappelling)
- ☐ Ropes (small)
- ☐ Shovel
- ☐ String
- ☐ Saw
- ☐ Tent
- ☐ Tin snips
- ☐ Whetstone
- ☐ Whistle
- ☐ Wire

Cooking Equipment

- ☐ Baking tins
- ☐ Barbecuing equipment
- ☐ Camp stove and fuel
- ☐ Dutch oven
- ☐ Grill
- ☐ Heat-proof gloves

□ Kettles   □ Reflector oven
□ Mixing bowls   □ Wire rack
□ Muffin pan

Kitchen Tools
□ Can opener   □ Spatula
□ Knives   □ Spoons
□ Measuring equipment   □ Toasting forks
□ Peeler   □ Turners

Kitchen Supplies
□ Basic condiments and   □ Napkins
   staples   □ Newspapers
□ Charcoal briquets   □ Paper plates, cups, bowls
□ Dishcloths and towels   □ Paper towels
□ Foil   □ Plastic bags
□ Garbage bags   □ Scrub pads
□ Hangers   □ Soap
□ Lighter fluid   □ Storage containers
□ Liquid soap (biodegradable)   □ Table cover
□ Matches

Clothing
□ Coat   □ Shirts
□ Gloves   □ Shoes (two pair: one for
□ Hat   hiking)
□ Jacket, sweater or sweatshirt   □ Socks (lightweight and
□ Pajamas   wool)
□ Pants (long)   □ Underclothing
□ Rain equipment

Sleeping Equipment
□ Ground cloth   □ Pillow
□ Insulated sleeping pad   □ Sleeping bags

Personal Items
□ Comb   □ Suntan lotion
□ Feminine hygiene products   □ Toilet paper
□ Insect repellent   □ Toothbrush
□ Lip balm   □ Toothpaste
□ Mirror   □ Towel and washcloth

Miscellaneous
- [ ] Camera and film
- [ ] First-aid kit
- [ ] Medicine (Rx and over-the-counter)
- [ ] Musical instrument
- [ ] Pocketknife
- [ ] Sunglasses

CHAPTER 4

Campsite

L ike building a home, planning an outdoor living area is a creative and meaningful experience. Many of the considerations are parallel, except that a campsite is temporary so your plans must include removing every trace of your stay. Remember these mottoes:

- Plan to meet your needs, but do not change the beauties of nature.
- Leave an area better than you found it.
- Leave nothing but tracks, and take nothing but pictures.

Selection of Campsite

To use out-of-the-way camping areas, whether they are public or private, it's important that you obtain permission from landowners or government agencies. Select a campsite using the following criteria.

Suitability

Are there places for a kitchen area, a fire area, toilet facilities and an area for sleeping? Whenever possible, investigate the campsite ahead of time to assess its facilities, or at least arrive early enough to set up camp before it gets dark.

Protection

Your first considerations should be the safety of the individual campers and protection of the natural beauty found at the campsite. Place tents and camping equipment on high ground in case of unexpected floods. Use existing vegetative screenage to provide protection and privacy.

From Wind

Wind tearing at the flaps of your shelter can create a miserable experience for you. Whenever possible, find a campsite hidden from the prevailing direction of the wind. Wind will not only intensify the cold, it can make your tent a noisy, flapping place, making it difficult for you to sleep.

SPECIAL EQUIPMENT TIPS FOR CAMPING WITH KIDS

I t is important when camping with small children to make your campsite a safe and recognizable place. Make a family flag or banner from brightly colored material and put it on top of your tent or hang it from a nearby tree to make it easy for your child to identify your campsite. Or, tie a noisy bell to the zipper or opening flap of your tent. If a child tries to leave the tent in the middle of the night, the bell will immediately alert you.

Warn your children about dangers, such as poisonous plants or hazardous areas. Reinforce their knowledge by having them draw their own pictures.

From Insects

One of the most tormenting experiences for campers is to be attacked by insects. Your shelter should be as nearly airtight as possible with insect-proof-size holes in netting. The following suggestions may help you avoid an insect-infested area:

- **Avoid damp areas.** Insects breed in moist habitats. The drier your campsite, the freer from insects you will be.
- **Search for a breeze.** Insects don't like breezes. If you can find a site with a constant movement of air, your chances of avoiding an insect onslaught are better.

From Bears

If you are in bear country, don't take any chances. Don't believe anyone who assures you "the bears around here are tame."

- **Put food out of reach.** Store food outside the tent, and have it high enough that a bear can't reach it, and far enough away from camp that the bear won't associate it with your camp.
- **Eat outside.** If possible, refrain from eating in your tent, where the odor of food will linger and invite a bear's curiosity. Food odor also clings to clothing; bring along several changes of clothing. If you are a woman, don't use perfume, and keep clean during your menstrual cycle.

- **Do not feed bears.** Once fed, a bear will come searching for more food. If you're asleep and unable to grant his desires, he may become dangerous.

From Cold

If you dress in lightweight layers, you'll sleep more warmly than in one heavy piece of clothing (although too many layers will prevent your body from warming the bag). Do not sleep in clothes you have worn. They tend to have body moisture, which can make you cooler on a cold night. Add padding between you and the ground, and take care to pitch your tent where it will receive the morning sun and warm the inside of your shelter.

From Fire

Common sense will probably tell you to avoid burning dry pine boughs or weeds that will shoot sparks toward your tent. Be careful when building a fire on a windy day. Pitch your tent so the wind won't blow fire and sparks in its direction.

Provisions

Is the site near water and dry wood? If it isn't, make special arrangements to bring them in. It is usually a good idea to take your own wood and charcoal briquets for cooking.

Sleeping Area

For sleeping, choose a smooth, flat area, free from bumps, roots and immovable rocks. Always choose a spot where you are protected from the elements by the natural surroundings (trees, bushes), or use coverings made with plastic or ponchos.

Don't choose an area that will collect drainage from rains or a swampy or moist area where there are numerous mosquitoes. Be careful to keep away from dead, overhanging branches, rotten trees or loose rocks on hillsides or rock walls. Falling trees or rocks can give a camper an unpleasant — or dangerous — wake-up call.

Kitchen

In the outdoor kitchen, as indoors, everything will run more smoothly if there is a basic organization with specific areas for performing all duties. The kitchen might include a cooking area, food storage areas for both refrigerated and staple foods, an equipment area, food preparation and eating areas, and a cleanup area.

Cooking Area

An essential part of camping is planning and establishing the cooking area. Many established campsites have built-in fire areas. If you are camping in an area where no fire area is established, get permission to prepare one. See chapter five for a complete course in fire building.

CONSERVATION

Choose a site where camp activities won't harm the natural beauty of the land. Special precautions should be taken to assure that no one carves trees, picks wildflowers or cuts green trees or branches. Do not destroy a natural habitat, follow already established trails, and choose a campsite where sparks from the fire won't spread or endanger vegetation.

Storage of Food

Staple Foods

Food requires protection from small animals and insects. Wooden boxes (usually heavy) with tight-fitting lids work well, as does either a box or a sack hung from a tree limb. Plastic containers are excellent for storing staples. If rodents are a problem, place the food in a bag, tie a knot in the rope, slip a can above the knot and hang it from a tree. This will prevent rodents from crawling down the rope into the stored food (Figure 4-1).

One of the best ways to organize a food supply for a group is to use a tent. Inside the tent everything should be placed in tight containers—plastic or cardboard—sturdy enough to keep rodents out. Food items can then be organized according to particular needs for each meal or by category, such as spices and seasonings, canned goods and mixed ingredients. The organiza-

Figure 4-1.
Box for storing
staple foods

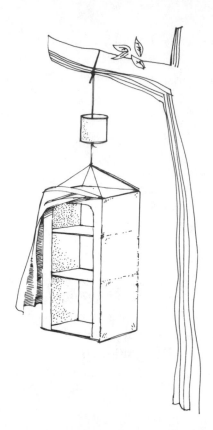

Figure 4-2. Creek refrigerator

tion should be clear enough that the cooks can easily find what they need.

Perishable Foods

One of these three types of refrigerators should suit your needs.

1. *Creek.* The refrigerator may simply be a shady, shallow spot at the edge of the creek (Figure 4-2). Here perishables can be placed in the cool water in a burlap sack, a wooden crate or a 5-gallon plastic bucket. The container should be anchored by placing rocks in and around it, and by tying it to a tree or a large rock at the edge of the creek or stream.

Figure 4-3.
Hanging portable burlap cooler

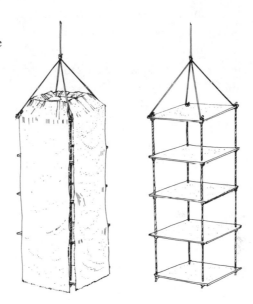

2. *Burlap cooler.* A hanging, portable cooler can be made from burlap, ¼- to ½-inch plywood and rope (Figure 4-3). Cut three or more squares of plywood into 2-foot squares (or the size desired). Drill holes the width of a small rope in each corner, then thread the rope through the corner holes. Tie knots the distance desired between the shelves. Hang the shelves by the rope ends from a tree (in a cool, shady place) and cover them with burlap. The front should be overlapped so that the burlap can be separated for access. Extend the burlap above the top of the cooler sufficiently to be immersed in a pan of water that sits on the top shelf. The burlap should

be stapled or attached to all edges of the shelves except in the center front. If the burlap is saturated with water to begin with and the top edges of the burlap are kept in a pan of water, it will stay wet by absorption and will be an effective cooler because of evaporation. (This does not work well in humid climates.)

3. *Cooler.* A commercial cooler in which either ice or dry ice is used is handy and effective. Items such as drinking water in milk cartons, juices or soft drinks can be frozen and placed in the cooler. Do not freeze liquid in glass bottles; they will break. When freezing liquid or any item in a container, leave room at the top for the liquid to expand when it freezes. Milk may be frozen to help keep the box cool although the freezing process separates the protein and changes the flavor somewhat. Shake the milk well before drinking. Commercial ice or "blue ice" can also be purchased for coolers. Before you go camping, freeze any meat that you plan to use two to three days into the camping trip. Dry ice will also keep items frozen. When using dry ice, always handle it wearing gloves and do not put it in an enclosed container. There must be a place for the carbon dioxide to be released. To locate vendors who sell dry ice, look in your Yellow Pages under the heading "Ice."

Storage Hints

For storage of particular items, follow these suggestions:

- If cheese is to be stored for a long period of time, wrap it in cheesecloth dipped in vinegar to reduce mold.
- Place a piece of apple, lemon or orange inside a covered container of brown sugar to keep the sugar soft.
- Prevent salt from lumping in humid climates by placing rice in the salt shaker. The rice will absorb the moisture and keep the salt dry.
- Place sugar, powdered sugar and salt and pepper in large salt shakers with lids. Before traveling, unscrew the lids, place plastic wrap over the shaker, and screw the lid over the wrap. This prevents the contents from spilling. In camp, remove the wrap. Be sure the shakers are either labeled or color coded to indicate their contents.
- If bananas or avocados are green, store them in brown paper

bags. The gases given off by the fruit will speed ripening.

- Many foods can be measured and prepackaged before leaving home. Prepare ahead of time the necessary quantities of muffin and biscuit mix, blending all ingredients except liquid and eggs.
- Store dry bread crumbs in plastic containers or plastic bags to use for augmenting meat and egg dishes. Use pastry crumbs or cake crumbs as toppings for puddings and desserts.
- Store eggs in styrofoam egg containers or break them into a quart jar or plastic container with a tight seal. They will pour out one at a time. If the plastic container has a spout, the eggs will come out of the spout one at a time. Use them within four days and keep them cool at all times. Eggs should be stored in the cooler. If you store eggs with the large end up, they will stay fresh longer. To check for freshness, place the egg in water. If it sits at the bottom of the pan, it's fresh. If it rises and floats in the water, the egg has lost moisture and its freshness.
- Place bread in a shoe box or plastic container to keep it from being smashed.
- Items purchased in glass jars should be placed in plastic containers so they won't get broken in travel.
- Buy butter or margarine in plastic containers for convenient use.

Food Preparation Area

Many campsites have tables available that can be used for preparing food. If a table is not available, spread a tarp on a flat rock or on the ground. Keep the area organized and clean as you work. Return all supplies to their storage area when they are no longer needed. Rinse all dishes used in preparing food before the food dries and becomes difficult to remove.

Eating Area

If a table is not available, select a shady spot and spread out a large piece of plastic or an army poncho. To add a special touch, prepare a centerpiece for the eating area. People often enjoy the warmth and informality of eating around the campfire. A large log can be used for seating, or a special log bench can be constructed, following these steps:

- Saw two 5- to 8-inch (in diameter) logs about 2 feet long.
- Cut a groove in the top of each of these logs so that another log can rest in the grooves without rolling.
- Place the small wedged logs on each end of the long log you will use as a seat (Figure 4-4).

Figure 4-4. Log bench

Cleanup Area

The cleanup area is important for health and sanitation. Efficient cleanup procedures save time and prevent unnecessary cleanup work.

Helpful Hints

- Soap the outsides of all pans before using them on an open fire. Use liquid detergent or soap lather. This will make it easier to wash the black build-up off the pans.
- When using sugar, line your cooking equipment with foil to make cleanup easier.
- Use paper towels to wipe dishes and to wipe the grease out of pans before washing them with water.
- Put the dishwater on to heat before the meal begins. Gallon cans work very well for heating water.
- If a pan is hard to clean, put water in it and let the water boil to soften the food particles.
- Use salt or sand to clean off still-warm cast-iron grills.

LAUNDRY

Camping or traveling is more enjoyable if you can slip into a change of clothes, freshly washed, when you begin to feel grubby. Have fun with these "washers," then devise one of your own, if you feel so inclined.

Agitating washer. Make a portable, agitating washer with any tall, waterproof container: a clean garbage can, a 2-gallon ice cream container (it may be either plastic or metal), or others. (See "Constant Hot Water" on the following page for ways to heat water for your wash.)

- Cover the soiled clothing with water and soap, leaving space at the top for the action of the plunger.
- Using a new or a clean toilet plunger, agitate the clothing with up-and-down and round-and-round motions in the water.

Traveling washer. If you're traveling, you can do your washing in a sealed container.

- Cover the clothing with water and add soap.
- Seal the container and place it in your car where it won't tip over, and preferably in the back of the trunk where the greatest agitation can be achieved.
- Line the container with a sealed, plastic garbage bag if the container doesn't have its own lid. The bumpier the road, the more "heavy-duty" the agitation. A smooth ride will provide only gentle washing, and additional hand scrubbing may be required to really clean your clothes.

Washing Dishes

There are several ways to do dishes on a camping trip. Select the one that best fits your needs and your environment. Soapy hot water is important for getting dishes clean. If the water is not clean enough to drink, add a little liquid bleach to the dishwater or boil the rinse water and dip dishes into it to kill any germs.

A cloth or net bag may be made to hold a camper's dishes while they are sterilized in boiling water. A drawstring should be pulled around the top of the bag so the bag can be closed before it's dropped into the water. Afterwards, the bag may be tied to a rope, which has been stretched between trees or to the limbs of a tree so that the dishes may dry.

Constant Hot Water

With a 5-gallon square can and a long-necked funnel you can construct a hot-water tank. Poke a hole in the side of the can large enough to allow the neck of the funnel to go all the way into the can. The funnel should be placed in the exact spot shown in the diagram so it will be far enough away from both the spout and the fire (Figure 4-5). Place the can on its side, filled with water up to its original opening, and place the tank in the hot coals near the fire. When you need a cup of hot water, place an empty container under the spout. Pour a cup of cold water through the funnel. One cup of hot water will come out.

Figure 4-5. Hot water tank

Storage of Equipment

Hanging Equipment Bag

A hanging bag with see-through sections is effective for storing equipment such as paper plates, napkins and utensils. Items can be categorized and placed in each see-through section. The sections can be stitched or partially stitched at one end to keep equipment from sliding out. The vinyl covering keeps equipment dry when it rains.

Equipment Rack

An equipment rack can be improvised from a man's traveling suit bag that zips in the front and is about 4 inches deep. Pockets designed to hold various types of equipment can be constructed. Equipment can be transported easily and will remain organized and clean in this type of container.

Equipment Box

A wooden box can become a permanent equipment storage place (Figure 4-6). One side swings down from the top and becomes the front opening, held on each side by a chain so it also can be used as a table. On each bottom corner of the box a molding is secured to hold the end of a pipe that becomes one of four legs to keep the box at working level. Holes are drilled in the sides near the top of the box to slide the pipes through so the box can be stored or carried. The pipes should be longer than the width of the box so they can be used as handles.

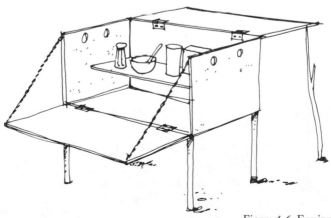

Figure 4-6. Equipment box

Plastic Boxes

An efficient way to store camping equipment year round is to use plastic boxes, about 20 by 30 by 18 (width × length × height). This system will speed up your ability to get away quickly. Label each box accordingly:

- **Staples:** aluminum foil, plastic wrap, paper towels, matches, toilet tissue, salt/pepper and other spices, syrup, coffee creamer, soup mixes, paper cups and plates, insect repellent, measuring cups, napkins, reusable plastic bags, garbage bags, hot cocoa mix, can opener, collapsible canteen and tablecloth.
- **Cooking Supplies:** hot pads, steel wool pads, knives, spatula, tongs, silverware, cutting board, cookie racks, dish towels, frying pans, pots and dish soap.
- **Tools:** flashlight, lantern, saw, hatchet, shovel, pliers, screwdriver, batteries, rope and first-aid kit.

Put all empty tubes, cans, paper towels, cardboard and so on in a large plastic bag when you run out and you'll know what needs to be purchased and put back into the plastic containers. Replenish boxes immediately upon your return and store boxes in an easy-access spot in your garage or storage room.

Equipment Area

Every piece of camping equipment should have a special place for its storage—"A place for everything and everything in its place." There are some good general rules to follow in the use and storage of camping equipment:

- **Safety first.** Have a chopping or sawing area where these kinds of equipment are to be used. Keep other people a safe distance away while you are cutting or sawing wood. Take precautions against the ax's slipping and cutting your leg or the saw's tearing your fingers. When you use a knife, always cut away from yourself. Be careful with equipment that contains kerosene or other liquid fuels; follow the directions on their labels.
- **Proper use.** Use the proper tool for the proper job. Don't abuse equipment by stabbing a knife into the ground in place of using digging equipment such as a shovel or using the side of the ax to pound pegs.

RECYCLING WHILE ROUGHING IT

Many communities now require recycling of paper, aluminum and plastic products. There may even be recycling provisions at your camping area. It's a good idea to check with local authorities regarding trash regulations.

Even if there are no particular rules governing recycling in your camping area, here's an easy way for environmentally conscious campers to recycle while roughing it:

- Take three or four white kitchen garbage bags and label them according to the recyclable material that will go into them (plastic, paper, etc.).
- Place these bags into a large, brown leaf bag labeled "recycle," and pack them with the other household items for the camping trip.
- At the campsite, hang the white, labeled garbage bags from the small, lower limbs of a tree close to the eating or garbage area. During cleanup, have a person responsible for separating and bagging recyclables.
- As you pack to leave, gather the filled white bags and twist-tie them closed. Put these bags into the large brown leaf bag for the journey home where you can deposit the items in the proper community recycling bins.

- **Proper repair.** Repair broken equipment before putting it away when you return from a trip so it will be ready to use when needed. Do not use damaged equipment. You may break it beyond repair. Keep cutting equipment sharp and in good repair for good service.
- **Proper storage.** Always place saws, axes, hatchets and knives in their proper storage places when they're not in use. To prevent rust from forming on the metal parts of equipment, cover all cutting blades or metal parts with sheaths or wrap them in heavy canvas when they're not in use. Find storage places that will allow you to keep this equipment off the ground and well protected from moisture. Be careful not to store gas- or oil-filled equipment in places where it can contaminate or be a safety hazard. Clean all equipment before you store it.

Bathroom Area

Keeping clean can be a real challenge when camping, but hygiene is still extremely important. There are several fun ideas in this section that will simplify your daily routine. Whenever you wash yourself or your clothes, be sure to use biodegradable soap, and do all washing (including brushing your teeth) far enough away from any lake or stream to keep wash water from flowing back in.

Grooming Apron

If you have trouble finding a convenient place in camp to put grooming items for brushing your teeth and combing your hair, make a handy apron for personal items. Not only will your gear be more organized, but you'll be less likely to drop your toothbrush in the dirt!

Take a bath towel, fold up the lower edge about 5 inches, and sew pockets to hold items such as toothpaste, soap, razor, comb, mirror and washcloth. Sew a casing about 2 inches above the pockets and thread a drawstring through it, making it long enough to tie around your waist.

The excess material at the top of the towel becomes a flap to keep the items from falling out of their pockets, and can also serve as a towel for drying your hands and face.

Figure 4-7. Using a grooming apron as a towel

Water Spout

Take a large, plastic bleach bottle with an airtight lid and poke a small nail hole in the front near the bottom to make a spout. Fill the bottle with water. When you are ready to wash your hands, loosen the lid and the pressure from the top will force a small stream of water from the spout. To create a larger stream of water from the jug, poke the hole with a golf tee. Then tie the upper part of the tee to the jug handle to use as a stopper.

Attach a rope to the handle and tie the jug to a tree limb. Place a bar of biodegradable soap in a nylon stocking, and hang it from the handle of the jug. Paint a face on it with the mouth over the spout area and you'll smile every time you use it!

Figure 4-8. Water spout

Outdoor Shower

If you hesitate to go camping because you're afraid you'll have to do without your daily shower, fear no more. This one is quick and simple to put together, and it works beautifully.

To make a shower room, you'll need an umbrella (without a sharp point), two shower curtains and some rope. Open the umbrella and turn it upside down, then tie one end of the rope to the umbrella handle. Throw the other end over a tree limb and loosely tie it to the tree trunk so that the umbrella is at eye level.

Hook the holes in the curtains onto the prongs of the umbrella, and raise the umbrella so that when a camper is standing under it, the bottom of the shower curtain is off the ground. Now tie the rope securely to the tree.

For water, purchase a new insecticide sprayer and mark the outside to read "CAMPING ONLY." Never use anything that once contained chemicals. If possible, buy a black can or paint it black.

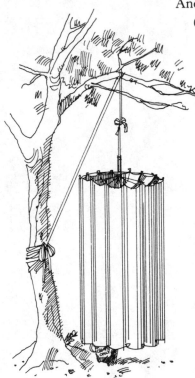

Another option is a "Sun Shower" (made by Basic Designs), a flat plastic bag, clear on one side and black on the other with a handle, sprinkler head and shut-off valve.

Plan ahead. Leave your water in the sun during the day for a heated afternoon shower.

The shower room is also a good place to change clothes. It can even be set up for the kids to play house while they are enjoying the outdoors.

Figure 4-9. Outdoor shower

Weatherproof Toilet Paper

To weatherproof a roll of toilet paper, you'll need a lightweight wire clothes hanger, a medium-sized coffee can with a plastic lid, and some tape.

With tin snips, cut and remove a ½-inch wide strip that runs from the top to the bottom of the can. Use tape to cover the raw edges of the slit.

On the bottom of the can, measure about 4½ inches away from the slit. Punch a hole close to the edge and large enough to insert the end of a wire clothes hanger. Punch a similar hole in the plastic lid.

Cut the bottom of the hanger in the middle and insert the ends through the holes. Tape the wires together so that they overlap nearly the length of the can.

Lift the plastic lid to insert a roll of toilet tissue, and feed the paper through the slit.

The coat hanger serves as a handle for carrying the tissue holder as well as a hook for hanging it on the branch of a tree.

Figure 4-10. Weatherproof toilet paper holder

Nighttime Toilet Paper Holder

If you have trouble finding the toilet paper in the dark and keeping it dry, try this nifty toilet paper flashlight holder. Remove the cardboard from a roll of toilet paper, and pull the paper out from the center (so the roll doesn't rotate). Place a flashlight and the toilet paper in a gallon-sized, self-sealing plastic bag. Pull the toilet paper (from the center) so that it hangs outside the bag and partially zip it up. In the middle of the night, you can turn on the flashlight and let it shine right through the bag.

Sanitation

One of the obligations of a camper or hiker is to see to proper waste removal, for your own protection as well as that of others. It is best to use available facilities wherever they exist, but out in the wild, you may not have access to such luxuries.

Urine poses few problems for the camper or the environment, other than odor. It evaporates quickly and contains few organisms that can transmit diseases.

Solid human waste is another matter, and extreme care should be taken for its proper disposal. Feces left on or near the ground surface, especially anywhere near water, can pollute an astonishingly large area. Even when the amount of waste is very small and buried, bacteria carrying disease can travel a good distance through the surrounding soil.

Before setting out on a camping or backpacking trip, always check on the disposal method recommended for the area you'll be visiting. The best alternative for solid waste disposal—one endorsed by the national park services and environmentalists, and the *only* alternative in many high-use areas and waterways— is to "pack it out." Empty ammunition cans and double or triple plastic bags are frequently recommended as suitable containers. A "Porta-John" or other portable privy is another choice. The Deluxe Water/Sanitation Kit (available from Emergency Essentials, Inc., 800-999-1863) is water storage and a portable toilet in one compact unit. You can store five gallons of water in the metalized plastic bag inside the sturdy box. When you need a toilet, remove the water bag, cut out the marked toilet seat and add the sanitary toilet bag. A good rule of thumb for all outdoor lovers is "when in doubt, pack it out."

Where digging is permitted, a latrine is probably the best solution if you plan to use one spot for several days. Pick a site at least 200 feet away from campsites, waterways (whether water is running or not) and established trails, but try not to pick a spot that might appeal to another party as a bed or picnic site.

If you are going to need a latrine, dig it immediately when you arrive at your campsite. Preserve the sod, and dig a narrow, shallow trench, no more than a foot and a half deep and a foot wide. If you need more capacity, make it longer, not deeper. If you go down below the topsoil into inert-looking earth, microorganisms cannot properly decompose the organic material.

After each use, throw in fresh soil or ashes. With large groups, you should also use lime (available at a garden store) to counteract odors, keep flies away and hasten decomposition. Completely fill the hole and restore the sod before leaving the campsite.

The single-use "cat hole" is recommended for individuals or small groups. Select sites using the same guidelines given for a latrine, and scatter the holes so that there will not be a concentration in one place. Dig a small hole 6 to 8 inches deep. Fecal matter buried too deep will not come in contact with helpful bacteria that break it down; buried too shallow, it will wash away with the first rainstorm, often into lakes and streams, or will become an attraction for flies and other insects. After use, tamp dirt into the hole, completely filling it, and restoring the area to its natural appearance.

Toilet paper may be the single most objectionable aspect of the human waste problem because it lasts a lot longer than fecal material. If buried or left, it deteriorates slowly, leaving telltale signs for months, even years. Put it into a small plastic bag to burn when the fire is not being used for cooking.

Do not bury any other trash, including tampons, sanitary napkins or diapers, which decompose even more slowly than toilet paper and whose odors assure that animals will dig them up. Dispose of diaper waste as you would any other fecal waste, and NEVER wash diapers in streams or lakes.

Leaving a Campsite

All of us like to arrive at a clean campsite. It is only good manners to leave it clean for the next campers.

Use only designated fire areas if possible. If you are in an undeveloped area where fire building is allowed and you have built your own fire area, restore it to its natural state. All fireplace rocks and other stones should be removed.

Any shelves or poles lashed to trees should be removed. Take all lashing twine with you.

All cans, tinfoil and even organic garbage should be disposed of in the garbage can or packed out.

A fun idea, especially for families with children, is for each person to pretend to be a "spy" as you're breaking camp. Can anyone find a sign that your family has been there? This fun game will assure that you always leave your campsite in a better condition than you found it!

CHAPTER 5

Fire Building

Fire building is a skill that may save your life. There's also no substitute for the cozy warmth of a campfire. With the need to preserve our wilderness areas, we must also be increasingly sensitive to environmental issues. Fire building is one aspect that requires thoughtful concern and care. One campfire ring provides cheery comfort and a delightful social atmosphere. A hundred campfires represent a blight on the landscape.

Before you decide on a campsite, find out what the fire regulations and recommendations are for the area. It is always wise to go prepared to cook on a camp stove and, where permitted, to use your campfire for sociability.

Campfire cooking definitely has its place, but many of the suggestions for campfire cooking in this book can be applied equally well to camp stove cooking. Most county, state and federal campsites have fire rings to encourage and contain your campfires. These rings are excellent for campfire cooking and do not cause damage to the environment, so use them when available.

When you are not camping in an officially designated campground, the following information will provide you with guidelines for doing your part to preserve the environment.

Fire building is acceptable when:

- You bring your own wood or you know there is an abundance of downed wood
- A fire site already exists and is in a good location
- You take appropriate safety precautions

Take your fire building equipment with you: a shovel, fire grate and water bucket. Whenever possible, bring your own wood.

For building the fire, select a spot at least 15 feet from trees, bushes and fallen trees. Fires built over roots are dangerous because the fire can follow the roots back to the trees or bushes and cause fires. Never build a fire directly under branches or near dry grass or weeds.

If you are not building your fire in the concrete rings provided in most campgrounds, use large rocks to enclose the fire. Analyze the area for the best location or any spots that may have already been used for a fire. It is better to have one well-built fire ring than several makeshift ones littering the area.

Always be aware of wind speed and direction. Sparks can travel great distances and smoke can annoy your neighbors.

Only build a fire large enough to satisfy your needs. Big fires are not required for cooking. Too much heat makes it difficult to control the cooking temperature. Most cooking is best done on hot coals or charcoal briquets rather than on direct flames.

The ideal is to always bring in your own wood, but if you're using wood from the campsite, take care not to burn larger downed branches that may be homes for small animals, birds and insects.

Never leave a fire unattended, and always have a bucket of water and a shovel near the fire to extinguish it in case it gets out of control. Put out your fire completely by drowning it with water. Stir the ashes to be sure that every ember is out before leaving your campsite. Whenever possible, haul out your ashes. Restore the area to its natural state.

Types of Wood

The three basic types of wood are tinder, kindling and fuel.

Figure 5-1. Tinder, kindling and larger logs

Tinder

For material to start the fire, use anything that will burn and is smaller than your little finger. Some examples of tinder are dry grass, dry leaves, small twigs, dry pine needles, fine shavings and bark.

Good tinder can be prepared at home in cardboard egg cartons. Save the lint from your dryer and fill the pockets of a cardboard egg carton with the lint. Then set the egg carton on a section of newspaper. Next, heat paraffin wax in a double boiler and pour the wax over the lint. Each time you need a fire starter, break off a pocket of the egg carton. It will burn for 10 to 15 minutes. Cotton balls soaked in paraffin also make good fire starting materials.

Figure 5-2. Tinder prepared in an egg carton

Kindling

Kindling is wood that ranges in diameter from the size of the little finger to the size of the wrist. It is used to feed the fire until larger pieces of wood begin to burn.

Fuel

Pieces of wood the size of the wrist and larger are classed as fuel. This type of wood is used to sustain the fire.

Building an A-Frame

The A-frame is the basic way to start all fires. It is also a perfect way to organize the tinder so you will ensure a successful fire. Follow these simple steps to make an A-frame.

- In the center of the fire-circle, start with three sticks approximately 1 inch in diameter and a foot long. Make a triangle by placing one end of each stick so that it overlaps another stick, with the other end resting on the ground.
- In the center of the A-frame, make a tepee with tinder, starting with very fine materials and graduating to larger pieces. Place some kindling around the tepee (Figure 5-3).
- Over the A-frame, lay the type of fire structure you desire. Light the tinder while it's still accessible, even if the fire structure is not entirely laid.
- Lay the fire so that air can circulate between the materials. Without enough air, the fire won't burn. You can fan the smoldering fire with a paper plate to aid the circulation.

Types of Fires

Fires are generally named for the manner in which the wood is stacked.

Tepee
The tepee fire is a basic fire used to begin other fires. Lay the A-frame and the tinder. Then set the kindling and fuel on end in the form of a tepee (Figure 5-4). The high flames of this fire are good for one-pot cooking and for the reflector oven.

Log Cabin Fire
To get a good bed of coals, build the log cabin fire by forming a basic A-frame and a tepee of tinder, then placing logs around the tepee as if you were building a miniature log cabin. Gradually lay the logs nearer the center as you build the cabin. It will have the appearance of a pyramid, and coals will form quickly when the fire burns down (Figure 5-5).

Figure 5-3. Basic A-frame with tepee kindling

Figure 5-4. Tepee fire

Figure 5-5. Log cabin fire

Figure 5-6. Crisscross fire

Figure 5-7. Star fire

Figure 5-8. Keyhole fire configuration

Crisscross Fire

For a large, deep bed of coals for Dutch oven cooking or roasting, prepare a crisscross fire. After forming a basic A-frame and a tepee of tinder and kindling, place the logs on the fire in layers, one layer crossing the other. Leave a little space between each log for air to circulate (Figure 5-6).

Star Fire

This fire is sometimes called the *lazy man's fire* because as the logs burn down, they are simply pushed farther into the flames (Figure 5-7). This fire is useful for preparing one-pot meals. Use the basic A-frame and the tepee of tinder and kindling to begin the fire, then feed the long logs into the center as needed. It is also a good way to burn the wood for an evening fire.

Keyhole Fire

The keyhole is the best design for both a campfire and a cooking fire (Figure 5-8). It is the most efficient to use in cooking since there is a constant supply of fresh coals that you can rake in when the temperature drops. Build the fire in the circle area and draw hot coals for cooking from the circle into the lower part of the keyhole. The keyhole can also be formed using bricks to provide a stable place for a grill.

Figure 5-9. Bricks supporting a grate on the end of a keyhole fire

Methods of Starting a Fire

There are many ways to start a fire. Some of the more primitive may be fun for younger (and older) campers and can also be used in times of emergency.

Matches

The most common method of starting a fire is to use matches. They can be protected against moisture by dipping them into either paraffin or fingernail polish. After dipping the matches, place them in the grooves of a piece of corrugated cardboard to let them dry. Keep matches in a waterproof container.

Figure 5-10. Matches dipped in paraffin

Newspaper

Another method of starting a fire uses newspapers. Roll several newspapers tightly until they are 4 inches in diameter. (Ecology catalogs sell a nifty device that tightly rolls newspapers into logs.) Tape around the outside to hold the paper log together, and cut it into 1-inch sections with a band saw. Then place the rolls of paper in melted wax, letting the paper absorb as much wax as possible; remove and place on paper to cool.

Caution: When melting wax, use a double boiler so that the wax will not ignite. It has a low combustion point.

When the sections are ready to use, merely pull out about 10 inches of the center and use it for a fire-starter.

Figure 5-11. Strip of newspaper for tinder

In snow or at times when tinder is not available, uncoil the center of the newspaper, light it, and let the whole roll burn. Small pieces of newspaper can also be rolled into smaller rolls, tied with string and dipped in wax.

Figure 5-12. Waxed newspaper fire

Roughing It Easy

Flashlight Batteries and Steel Wool

A rather dramatic method of starting a fire is to conduct the electricity from two flashlight batteries through steel wool. Use 00 or a finer grade steel-wool roll, cut or tear it into a ½-inch strip (which will lengthen out to a strip 7 or 8 inches long), and two good flashlight batteries. Place one battery on top of the other, making sure both are in an upright position like they would go into a flashlight. Take one end of the strip of steel wool and hold it against the bottom of the lower battery.

Take the other end of the wool and rub it across the top of the top battery. After the steel wool sparks, place it next to the tinder and blow on it. This is a great way to get a fire going when the wind is blowing. You can touch the steel wool to both posts on a 9-volt battery and the fire will start instantly. Be sure to pack the steel wool and batteries in separate containers.

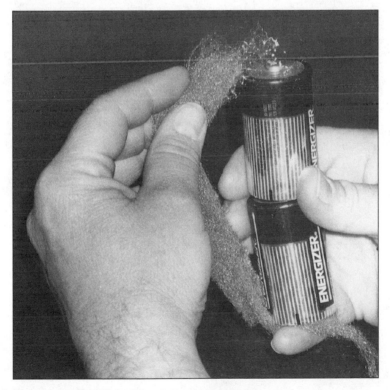

Figure 5-13. Flashlight batteries and steel wool

Flint and Steel

A meat-cutter's steel (piece of metal used to sharpen knives), a steel knife blade or a file struck against stone will cause sparks. The sparks will create a thin wisp of smoke if they come in contact with very dry tinder. When smoke appears, blow gently with short puffs of air until the tinder bursts into flame. Very fine tinder or charred cloth will facilitate ignition. A spark in very fine steel wool will also work.

Magnifying Glass

A strong magnifying glass placed in the direct sunlight so that a fine point of light is focused into dry tinder will cause the tinder to smoke and eventually break into flame.

Bow Drill

If constructed properly, a bow drill, consisting of a fireboard, drill, socket and bow, will create heat that can light tinder. Cut a notch in the side of a fireboard. Pass a drill through the notch and rest it on a flat, grooved surface (Figure 5-14). A hand-held socket, lubricated with grease, allows the drill, operated with the string of a bow, to rotate first one way and then another until a fine, hot dust results. When the dust becomes heated and begins to smoke, place it in the tinder and blow it into flame.

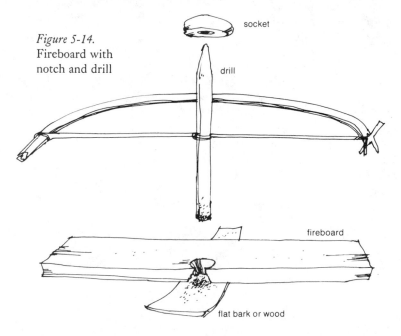

Figure 5-14.
Fireboard with notch and drill

socket

drill

fireboard

flat bark or wood

Roughing It Easy

Extinguishing a Fire

Knowing how to extinguish a fire properly is as important as, if not more important than, knowing how to start one. First, break up the fire with a stick and spread out the coals. Sprinkle water over the coals. Keep stirring the fire with the stick and drenching it with water until the coals are cool enough to touch. Don't suddenly pour a large amount of water on a hot fire. The steam might burn bystanders. A fire is not out until the coals are cool enough to touch. If large logs have been burning, make sure all the sparks are put out.

When Open Fires Are Not Permitted

In many camping areas open fires are illegal because of fire hazard. Increasingly, campers are forced to use other methods of heat for cooking food out of doors.

Tablets

Commercial tablets, available at camping-goods stores, can be placed in a small stove and lighted. These tablets are about 1 inch in diameter and about ½-inch thick. They are very good for warming canned food and other quick-cooking items. They may be used either with the tin-can stove or with a small commercial stove made expressly for their use. If a stove is not available, place stones closely around the tablets to serve as a stand to hold small cooking pots and cans.

Canned Heat

Canned heat can be used for cooking or warming food in cans. Special stoves made to use with canned heat may be purchased.

Paraffin

Make your own can of heat by rolling narrow strips of corrugated cardboard into a tuna-fish can and filling the can with melted paraffin. Step-by-step directions are in the section on the tin-can stove starting on page 83.

Newspapers

Newspapers can be used in the tall-can stove for cooking meat as shown in the section starting on page 91.

Charcoal Briquets

Charcoal is one of the best kinds of fuel to use when open fires are not permitted or when it is against the law for wood to be gathered. Charcoal briquets are good for grilling meat, for cooking foil meals, for spit or stick cooking, and for the Dutch oven. Charcoal briquets should never be burned in an enclosed area; doing this is extremely dangerous. Two rules to remember when you are using charcoal briquets:

1. Never light briquets with homemade lighting fluid or gasoline; they could explode.
2. Always allow 40-50 minutes for the briquets to become hot.

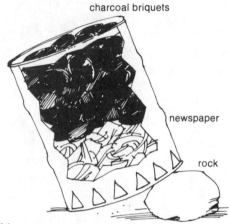

charcoal briquets

newspaper

rock

Figure 5-15. Chimney starter

A good way to shorten the heating time for charcoal briquets and to ensure an even heat is to use the chimney starter method (Figure 5-15). You can either buy one or make one following these steps. Using two or three sheets of newspaper, matches and a #10 tin can, follow these steps:

- Cut both ends out of the can.
- Punch holes every 2 inches around the lower edge of the can with a punch-type can opener.
- Set the can down so the holes are next to the ground.
- Crumple two or three sheets of newspaper. Wearing a glove to avoid cutting your hand, place them in the bottom of the can.
- Place charcoal briquets on top of the crumpled newspaper.
- Lift the can and light the newspaper. Prop a bottom edge of

the can on a rock to create a good draft. The briquets will be ready to use in 30 to 40 minutes.

- If a greater draft is necessary, prop the can on small rocks and fan the flames with a paper plate.
- When the briquets are hot, lift the chimney off the coals and spread the coals out. They are ready to use.

The chimney starter is also useful for more rapid heating of briquets when lighter fluid is used. The can will ensure an even heat for all the fuel.

Egg Carton Briquet Starters

Another way of lighting briquets is to use wax in a cardboard egg carton. Separate the lid from an egg carton and set the bottom of the carton inside the lid. A little wax poured inside the lid first will make the cupped half adhere to it. Then pour approximately ¼ inch of melted paraffin into each egg cup and let the wax cool. When it is cool, set a charcoal briquet in each cup, then continue to stack briquets over the carton. Light the carton and wait for the briquets to heat.

Starting Briquets Over a Campfire

Briquets can also be added to wood fires to provide a better and larger bed of coals. Pour the briquets into the hot fire and allow them to heat for 20 to 30 minutes. An effective way to start charcoal briquets over an open fire is to shape a screen (½- to ¾-inch mesh) into a bucket or bowl-shaped basket. Make a wire bale for lifting or carrying. Place the desired amount of charcoal briquets into the basket and set it over an open fire (Figure 5-16). If the fire is hot, particularly if there are good flames, the charcoal will start quickly, and it will all heat evenly.

Commercial Starters

Commercially prepared charcoal starters and jellies can be purchased. It is important that you put the right amount of the mixture on the briquets, then close the container of the starter and place it out of the way of sparks or flames before lighting the briquets.

Electric Starters

If electricity is available, it can be used to start the briquets. Place an electric coil in the fire bed and place the briquets over these.

Extinguishing Briquets

Use your briquets over and over again until they are burned out. Put them out by using one of the following methods:

1. Place them in a can that can be covered with a lid or with foil. The cover cuts off the oxygen supply, and the briquets will cease to burn.
2. Place them in a can of water. The briquets must be dry before being used again.

Figure 5-16. Portable basket of hot briquets

CHAPTER 6

Introduction to Outdoor Cookery

Preparing foods outdoors is especially satisfying because there are some aspects of cooking that cannot be duplicated in an indoor kitchen, particularly the addition of woodsmoke flavoring and fresh air. With a keen outdoor appetite, cool mornings and a warm fire, campers can enjoy a nutritious breakfast, a good lunch during their hike in the woods, and an evening meal by the campfire. For many, this would be the end to a perfect day.

The following carefully tested methods of preparing foods will add interest and variety to your whole camping experience. This chapter will give you ideas on how to adapt familiar indoor cooking methods and principles in the outdoors. Refer to the following list for outdoor methods that can be used to duplicate familiar indoor results. Then look for instructions in the following pages for a particular method of outdoor cooking to see what type of fire to build; the equipment you will need to gather, purchase or make; suggestions on foods to use; and step-by-step directions to follow. With the variety of easy ways of preparing foods available to you, camp cooking should never become dull or routine. A feeling of pride and satisfaction will accompany a well-prepared meal in the out-of-doors.

Indoor Cooking Methods Duplicated in Outdoor Setting

Bake: Cook With Dry Heat

Tin can stove

Dutch oven

Can oven

Reflector oven

Pit cooking

Food inside of food

Sand cooking

Barbecue: Cook Over Direct Heat and Season With Seasoned Sauce

Stick and spit   Tall can
Can barbecue

Boil: Cook With Water or Moisture

Aluminum foil   Liquid in paper cup
Tin can, billy can   Double boiler
Dutch oven

Braise: Sauté in a Small Amount of Fat, Then Cook Slowly in Covered Pan With Liquid

Frying pan   Dutch oven

Broil: Cook With Direct Heat

Can barbecue   Spit cooking
Stick cooking

Fry: Cook With a Small Amount of Fat

Aluminum foil   Dutch oven
Tin can stove

Roast: Cook With Dry Heat

Tin can stove   Reflector oven
Dutch oven   Pit cooking
Can oven

Steam: Cook With Moist Heat

Aluminum foil   Dutch oven

Stew or Slow Roast: Cook for a Long Time in a Small Amount of Liquid

Dutch oven   Pit cooking

Planning Meals Using Recipes

Meals at camp can be as interesting as they are at home if they are planned well. There are many factors to consider in planning for your group: tastes, costs, methods of cooking, duration of the camping trip, mode of transportation, number of people to cook for, and ages of the campers. If marketing sources are unavailable for a week, fresh produce and meat are concerns; if the trip entails backpacking, heavy items are impractical.

The key to planning good, practical meals for your camp is to choose your activities, and then plan your meals around those activities. For example, it is not good planning to have a breakfast that will take extra time to prepare if you want to start on an early hike.

Meals and Menus

The best guide available for planning daily menus is the food pyramid defined by the Department of Agriculture. If this food pyramid is followed, it will form a basis for general good health at camp. Include the required servings of each group daily.

- **Meat group:** two to three servings for energy and growth (meats, poultry, fish, eggs, cheese and legumes).
- **Dairy foods:** two for adults, three to four for children and teens for growth and body maintenance (milk, butter, cheese and other milk products).
- **Vegetables:** one or two dark green or yellow vegetables.
- **Fruits:** one or two citrus fruits or tomato. (Three or more servings of fruits and vegetables are recommended for good health.)
- **Breads and cereals:** six or more servings for body regulation (breads, breakfast cereals, macaroni or noodles and rice).

Nutrition is always important. Since outdoor activities require great amounts of energy, it is necessary that you carefully plan nutritious, well-balanced meals.

Breakfasts out-of-doors should be larger than other meals and full of energy foods. The lighter of the two remaining meals — lunch and dinner — could be a one-pot meal, a sack lunch or hot dogs on a stick. Dinner is important because by the end of a day of adventure, appetites are usually up.

Shopping

Use Charts

With careful planning beforehand, you can save shopping time and avoid wasting food. Purchase only those foods you have *planned* to use. The following three-step method should prove helpful to you.

- **Three-Day Meal Planner Chart:** Plan carefully the menu for each meal. (See page 73.)

- **Shopping Guide Chart:** From the menu, prepare a shopping guide of foods to be purchased. (See pages 74 and 75.)
- **Checklist for Food Chart:** Write the amounts of each food you will need for each meal on this checklist, which will serve as your market order. (See pages 76 and 77.)

Cooking Time

Learning the cooking time for foods (when foods are done but not burned) is difficult at first but becomes easier with experience. In general, foods cooked out-of-doors should take about the same amount of time as foods cooked indoors. Foods cooked too fast run the risk of being either burned or cooked on only one side or of remaining raw in the middle. The chart on pages 78-80 gives suggested cooking times and methods for recipes included in this book. The cooking time may vary according to amounts of food, altitude and the degree of heat in coals.

Types of Wood Cooking

The length of time will vary according to the type of wood you use. Hardwood from broad-leafed trees makes longer-lasting coals, providing a more extended cooking time than the soft-woods from needlelike, evergreen trees.

Altitude

Water boils at 212° F at sea level. For every 1,000 feet above sea level, the boiling temperature drops 2° F. At 5,000 feet, water boils at 202° F. Because of the lower boiling temperature at higher altitudes, foods take longer to cook.

Concentration of Coals

The amount and concentration or thickness of the bed of coals also determines the length of the cooking time. The more concentrated the coals, the shorter the time for cooking. Take care not to cook items faster than you would at home because this will often burn the food.

Substitutes

Sometimes, as careful as we are in shopping or packing, there are items missing from our supplies. It is helpful to know how to expand meat with eggs, onions and bread crumbs and how to expand eggs with bread crumbs. You should also learn what ingredients can be substituted for others. The suggestions in the following chart may prove useful:

- 1 teaspoon baking powder: ⅓ teaspoon baking soda plus 1 teaspoon cream of tartar
- 1 cup butter: 1 cup margarine
- 1 cup buttermilk or sour milk: 1 tablespoon vinegar or lemon juice in enough milk to make one cup; let stand for 5 minutes
- 1 oz. (square) chocolate: 3 tablespoons cocoa plus 1 tablespoon fat
- 1 tablespoon flour: ½ tablespoon cornstarch; 2 tablespoons quick tapioca
- 1 cup honey: 1¼ cup sugar plus ¼ cup liquid
- 1 cup milk: ½ cup evaporated milk plus ½ cup water
- 1 cup evaporated milk: 1 cup double-strength powdered milk
- 2 tablespoons onion: 1 tablespoon dried onion
- 1 cup white sugar: 1 cup brown sugar

Recipes

Because so many recipes are available to the public and adaptable to the outdoor setting, this book acquaints you instead with some basic "tried-and-true" recipes and with ideas to help you adapt your own recipes to outdoor cooking. Each recipe is broken down into six or seven parts:

- **Title.**
- **Cooking methods.** Many methods, including those you might create, may be used to cook the same item.
- **Cooking time.** The cooking time will vary greatly, so a rough estimate of the time is given, as well as a suggestion as to what constitutes "done" for each recipe. Check food often while you are learning.
- **Recipe yield.** The approximate number of servings is given.
- **Directions and ingredients.** Step-by-step directions are given

at the left; ingredients for each step are shown at the right.

- **Variations.** Many items can be added to change the recipe, or the basic recipe may be prepared in several different ways. This list is by no means exhaustive. Your imagination can add many more variations to each recipe.
- **Hints.** Along with some of the recipes, helpful suggestions are given.

The recipes are categorized into *breakfast*, *lunch* (the lighter meal of the day), *dinner* (meats, vegetables, salads, breads, beverages, desserts — these can be used in lunch menus also) and *snacks*.

Cooking Without Recipes

To prepare foods without following specific recipes, it may be helpful to keep a few points in mind.

- In creating your own stew, always remember to brown the onions and meat first, then add water and each vegetable according to its cooking time — carrots and potatoes first, then celery later.
- When you boil pastas (spaghetti, ravioli or any fresh dough) or rice, remember to use about two times as much water as pasta. Bring the salted water to a boil first and then add the pasta or rice. Add butter or oil to the boiling water so that the water will not boil over and so that the pasta will not stick together. Cover it and cook it at a low, bubbling temperature. For precooked rice, simply add rice to the boiling water, allow the water to return to a boil, then remove the pan from the heat and let it stand for about 5 minutes while the rice swells.
- Here are some general rules to follow: Use ½ teaspoon of salt for each pound of meat; 1 tablespoon of baking powder for every 2 cups of flour; ½ teaspoon of salt for each cup of flour; 2 tablespoons of flour for each cup of liquid (for medium thickening); ⅓ cup of powdered milk (instant) for each cup of water.

Never be afraid to try something completely different in your cooking — indoors or out.

THREE-DAY MEAL PLANNER

	First Day Breakfast	Second Day Breakfast	Third Day Breakfast
Protein Food			
Cereal and/or bread			
Fruit or juice			
Beverage			
Utensils			

	First Day Lunch	Second Day Lunch	Third Day Lunch
Main dish or salad			
Vegetable and/or fruit			
Bread			
Dessert			
Beverage			
Utensils			

	First Day Dinner	Second Day Dinner	Third Day Dinner
Main dish			
Vegetable			
Salad			
Bread			
Dessert			
Beverage			
Utensils			

SHOPPING GUIDE

Food	Weights/Approximate Measurement	Approximate Servings
Beverage		
Coffee singles	3.5 ounces	19 coffee bags
Hot chocolate	12 ounces	1 serving
Kool-Aid	1 package	8 servings
Soft drink	12 ounces	1 serving
Tea	3.5 ounces	16 tea bags
Bread		
1 loaf	1 pound	20 to 22 slices
Cereal		
Ready to eat		
Flaked	18 ounces/18 to 20 cups	18 to 20 1-cup servings
Puffed	18 ounces/32 to 36 cups	26 1½-cup servings
Cooked		
Oatmeal	18 ounces/6 cups (1 cup uncooked = 1⅔ cups cooked)	12 to 14 ¾-cup servings
Rice	1 cup uncooked	6½ cups cooked servings
Crackers		
Graham	1 pound/65 crackers	32 to 35 2-cracker servings
Saltine	1 pound/130 squares	32 4-cracker servings
Dairy Products		
Cheddar cheese	1 pound/12 to 16 slices 4 cups grated	6 to 8 sandwiches (2 slices each)
Cottage cheese	1 pound/2 cups	6 to 8 ¼-cup servings
Milk		
Evaporated	14½ ounces/1⅔ cups	Equivalent to 3⅓ cups milk. 1 can milk + 1 can water = whole milk
Whole	1 quart/4 cups	4 servings
Nonfat dry	1 pound/5 quarts	20 servings
Fats		
Butter or margarine	1 pound/2 cups	48 pats
Shortening	1 pound/2½ cups 3 pounds/7½ cups	
Salad oil	1 pint/2 cups	
Flour		
All-purpose	1 pound/4 cups	
Whole wheat	1 pound/3½ cups	
Fruit Juices		
Frozen concentrated	6 ounces/3 cups	6 ½-cup servings
Canned	46 ounces/5¾ cups	11 to 12 ½-cup servings
Fruits, Fresh		
Apples	1 pound/3 medium	3
Bananas	1 pound/3 medium	3
Grapefruit	1 pound/2 medium	2
Oranges	1 pound/2 medium	2 (1 orange = ⅓ cup juice)
Pineapple	2 pounds/1 medium	6 to 8

SHOPPING GUIDE (CONTINUED)

Food	Weights/Approximate Measurement	Approximate Servings
Meats		
Bacon	1 pound/20 to 24 slices	10 to 12 2-slice servings
Hamburger	1 pound/2 cups	4 to 5
General guide:		
Boneless meat	1 pound	4
Small-boned meat	1 pound	3
Large-boned meat	1 pound	2
Chicken	2½ to 3½ pounds	4
Ham	1 pound	4 to 6
Fish	1 pound	2
Pasta		
Macaroni	1 pound/4 cups uncooked	
	8 cups cooked	14 to 16 ½-cup servings
Noodles	1 pound/6 cups uncooked	
	8 cups cooked	14 to 16 ½-cup servings
Spaghetti	1 pound/4 cups uncooked	
	8 cups cooked	14 to 16 ½-cup servings
Sugar		
Brown	1 pound/2¼ cups packed	
Granulated	1 pound/2¼ cups	
Confectioners'	1 pound/4 cups	
Syrup		
Corn syrup	1 pint/2 cups	
Honey	1 pound/1¼ cups	20 1-tablespoon servings
Molasses	1 pint/2 cups	16 2-tablespoon servings
Pancake	1 pint/2 cups	16 2-tablespoon servings
Legumes, Dried		
All kinds	1 pound/2 cups uncooked	6 1-cup servings
	6 cups cooked	
Vegetables, Fresh		
Beans	1 pound/3 cups	5 to 6 ½-cup servings
Broccoli	1 pound	3 to 4 ½-cup servings
Cabbage:		
Raw	2-pound head/18 to 24 leaves	14 ½-cup servings
Cooked	2 pounds	8 ½-cup servings
Carrots	3 mature/2½ cups	5 ½-cup servings
Cauliflower	1 pound/1½ cups	3 ½-cup servings
Lettuce	1 pound/1 large head	8 to 10
Onions	3 large; 4 to 5 medium/2½ to 3 cups	
Potatoes	1 pound/3 medium	3
Tomatoes	1 pound/3 to 4	5 to 8
Micellaneous		
Marshmallows	1 pound/64	
Peanut butter	18 ounces/2 cups	8 to 10 2-tablespoon servings
Potato chips	1 pound	16
Walnuts	1 pound/4 to 4½ cups	8 ½-cup servings

CHECKLIST FOR FOOD

Beverages
_____ dairy drink
_____ hot chocolate
_____ coffee
_____ tea
_____ soft drink
_____ Kool-Aid
_____ fruit juices
_____
_____
_____ tomato juice
_____
_____

Bread and Cereal
_____ bread
cold cereal
_____
_____
cooked cereal
_____
_____

Canned Foods
fruits
_____
_____
meats
_____
_____
soup
_____
_____
vegetables
_____
_____

Dehydrated and Dried Foods
_____ eggs
_____ fruit
_____ meat
_____ onions
_____ potatoes
_____ soup
_____ vegetables
_____
_____
_____
_____
_____

Cleaning Products
_____ dish soap
_____ bath soap
_____ soap pads
_____ cleansers
_____
_____
_____

Condiments/Dressings
_____ catsup
_____ honey
_____ jam
_____ jelly
_____ mustard
_____ olives
_____ peanut butter
_____ pickles
_____ salad dressing
_____ vinegar
_____
_____
_____

Dairy Products
_____ butter
_____ buttermilk
_____ cheese
_____ cottage cheese
_____ eggs
_____ margarine
_____ milk
_____ sour cream
_____
_____
_____

Meat
_____ bacon
_____ beef
_____ chicken
_____ ground beef
_____ ham
_____ sausage
_____ steaks
_____ wieners
_____
_____
_____
_____
_____

CHECKLIST FOR FOOD

Produce

_____ apples
_____ bananas
_____ celery
_____ carrots
_____ cucumbers
_____ grapefruit
_____ green peppers
_____ lemons
_____ lettuce
_____ melons
_____ onions
_____ oranges
_____ potatoes
_____ tomatoes

Paper Products

_____ aluminum foil
_____ bathroom tissue
_____ garbage bags
_____ tissues
_____ paper cups
_____ paper plates
_____ paper sacks
_____ paper towels
_____ plastic bags
_____ plastic wrap
_____ waxed paper
_____
_____
_____

Miscellaneous

MEAL PLANNING AND COOKING TECHNIQUES

Numbers in this chart (except those labeled *hr.* or *hrs.*) refer to cooking time in minutes.	Stick	Spit	Tin Can Stove	Aluminum Foil	Tall Can Stove	Can Oven	Dutch Oven	Reflector Oven	Pit	Nonutensil	Novelty
Breakfast											
Eggs and Egg Variations											
Soft and Hard-Cooked							10-20				10-20
Fried		5	5				5				
White Sauce							10				
Creamed							15-20				
Scrambled			3-5	3-5			3-5				
Eggs in a Basket			5	5			5				
Poached							10-15				
Bacon and Egg in a Sack											5
Bacon on a Stick	3-5										
Cereal							varies				
Overnight Breakfast							over-night				
Pancakes			3-5	3-5			3-5				
Cinnamon Toast	3-5			3-5				3-5			3-5
French Toast			3-5				3-5	3-5			
Lunch											
Special Stew							2 hrs.				
Sloppy Joes							20				
Campfire Sandwich				10							
Pizza							15-20	20			
Minute Pizza				10-15			10-15	10-15			
Pig in a Blanket	10						10	10			
No-fuss Lunch							15-20				
Bac-o-cheese Dogs	10-15							10-15			
Frank-a-bobs	5-10	5-10									
Dinner											
Meats											
Meat Loaf on a Stick	15-20	15-20									
Cannonballs				15-20			15-20				
Bunyan Burgers				25							
Meat Loaf				varies			60		3 hrs.		
Quick Meat Loaf								15-20			

Numbers in this chart (except those labeled *hr.* or *hrs.*) refer to cooking time in minutes.	Stick	Spit	Tin Can Stove	Aluminum Foil	Tall Can Stove	Can Oven	Dutch Oven	Reflector Oven	Pit	Nonutensil	Novelty
Meat Loaf in Cabbage				20-30		20-30	20-30				
Hamburgers			5	5	5		5				
Steak			varies	varies	varies		varies			varies	
Stuffed Zucchini				20-25			20-25				
Foil Dinner				25							
Hamburger Stew							60				
Tacos			15				15-20				
Beef Stroganoff							20-30				
Quick Macaroni Casserole							20-30				
Shish Kebab	10-20	10-20									
Camp Stew							45-60				
Stuffed Pork Chops							1 hr.		3 hrs.		
Barbecued Spareribs		1-2 hrs.					1 hr.				
Chicken Dinners											
Dutch Oven Chicken Dinner							45-60				
Chicken in Dutch Oven							45				
Chicken on a Spit		2 hrs.									
Chicken in a Pit									3-4 hrs.		
Fish											
Fried				varies	varies		varies				
Baked						30-40	30-40				
Steamed				20-30			20-30				
Vegetables											
Fresh				varies			varies				
Canned							varies				
In Foil				varies							
Potatoes											
Baked				1 hr.			1 hr.		1-3 hrs.		
Boiled							45-60				
Fried							20				
Scalloped						40-50	40-50				
Roesti							10-20				
Corn on the Cob	15			10-15			10-15				

Numbers in this chart (except those labeled *hr.* or *hrs.*) refer to cooking time in minutes.	Stick	Spit	Tin Can Stove	Aluminum Foil	Tall Can Stove	Can Oven	Dutch Oven	Reflector Oven	Pit	Nonutensil	Novelty
Hot Pot Green Beans							20				
Fried Tomatoes			5-10				5-10				
Camp Chili							20-30				
Baked Beans							1½ hrs.				
New England Baked Beans							5-6 hrs.		5-6 hrs.		
Quick Breads											
Biscuits Supreme						10-15	10-15	10-15		10-15	
Muffins			15-20					15-20			
Bread Twist	varies	varies									
Indian Fry Bread							5				
Twisted Donuts and Holes							5	5			
Crêpes							3-5				
Yeast Breads											
Hot Rolls							15-20	15-20			
Desserts											
Fruit Kebab	3-5	3-5									
Chocolate Pudding Cake							40-50	60			
Baked Apples				45-60		45-60	45-60	45-60			
Fruit Dumplings						20-30	20-30	30			
Pioneer Cobbler						25-30	25-30	30			
Pineapple-upside-down Cake			20				30-45	30-45			
Brown Bears in an Apple Orchard							25-45	25-45			
Cake in an Orange				10-15			15-20	15-20			
Cherry Delight			20			20	20-30	30			
Graham Cracker Cherry Pudding						20-30	20-30	30			
Easy Brownies						30-40	30-40	40			
Snacks											
S'mores	2-3							3-5			
Banana Boat				5							
Shaggy Dogs	2-3										

CHAPTER 7

Direct-Heat Cooking

Direct heating is like the burner on your stove. Food is placed in a container that comes in direct contact with the heat. Equipment used for this kind of cooking can range from pots, pans and foil to wet paper and leaves. As kinds of food vary, so will the amount of heat and cooking time. Care should be taken not to use too many coals under items that cook better at lower heats.

Who Needs a Pot?

One of the best parts of outdoor cooking is being able to experiment with not only different cooking methods, but also different utensils. In camping, less is often more, so try these ideas for cooking without pots and pans.

Cooking in Clay
A wrapping of clay (if you are in an area where the soil is claylike) will protect food from too much heat as it cooks in a bed of coals.

- Wrap potato to be cooked in foil.
- Wrap 1 inch of clay around the potato.
- Bury it in the coals for 1 hour.
- Remove it, crack off the hardened clay, remove the foil and rinse the potato if necessary. Eat it immediately.

If the clay-wrapped article of food is cooked on *top* of the coals, you should double the cooking time, turning it over when half the time is up.

To hard-cook an egg, make a pinhole in its large end to relieve air pressure during the cooking. Cover the egg with clay and bury it in coals for 20 to 30 minutes. If it is placed on top of the coals, it may take as long as 40 to 45 minutes to cook. Remember to turn it over after 30 minutes if cooking the egg on top of the coals.

Figure 7-1. Cooking hamburger in a cabbage leaf

Cooking on Leaves

Large leaves, such as cabbage and lettuce leaves, may be used to cook meats (Figure 7-1). Be sure the leaf is edible (nonpoisonous).

- Season the meat and place it on the leaf.
- Place the leaf over the coals.

The outside edges of the leaf will become brown and limp, but the area under the meat will remain cooler and more moist; consequently, that part of the leaf will retain its body. Remove from coals and turn meat over to finish cooking.

Cooking in Paper

Food can be cooked in paper if the paper is wet before it is placed on the coals. Fish is the food best suited to this type of cooking.

- Place oiled fish on a piece of wet paper. A brown paper sack works very well.
- Wet one sheet of newspaper and roll the package in it.

The size of the package and the temperature of the coals will cause the cooking time to vary—10 to 15 minutes should be adequate. If you like this method, you may want to experiment with other foods. A paper bowl will also cook a hamburger. Set the bowl on a piece of foil and then onto the coals.

Heating Milk in Paper Cartons

Heating milk or milk products (including chocolate milk) in a pan can be a long (and sometimes not so successful) experience. Milk products scorch quickly and leave a hard-to-clean residue in the pan. Milk products purchased in nonwaxed cardboard containers can be heated quickly in the carton. This method shouldn't be used with a waxed carton.

- Wrap foil around the bottom of the carton to prevent the seam from burning and causing a leak.
- Open the top of the container so steam can escape as the product heats.
- Place the carton in the coals and leave it for a few minutes. Watch closely; it heats quickly.

Coffee-Can Cooking

One of the simplest methods of cooking with contact heat is to use an empty 29-ounce coffee can as a pot.

- Place food in layers in the can, seasoning it as you go. (Several different kinds of vegetables may be used, along with hamburger. A suggested combination is onion, carrots, potatoes, hamburger, potatoes, carrots and onion.)
- Cover the top of the can with heavy-duty foil.
- Place the can on medium-hot coals.
- Put coals on top of the foil.
- Cook for ½ hour to 45 minutes.
- Using heat-proof gloves, remove the can from the coals and serve a delicious meal.

Tin Can Stove

The tin can stove is not only one of the most pleasurable and innovative outdoor cooking methods, but it is also an excellent item to have in the home for emergencies and natural disasters.

Principle
With a tin can stove, heat is conducted to the top of a specially prepared gallon can where it can be used for frying, boiling or

Figure 7-2. Tin can stove

Figure 7-3. Rolled cardboard

Figure 7-4. Wax over a buddy burner

baking. The tin can stove is best used to prepare food for only one or two people because of the limited cooking surface (Figure 7-2).

Fire(s)

Two sources of heat may be used for the tin can stove: (1) a wood fire built under the can, and (2) a buddy burner (a tuna can—or a can similar in shape—full of rolled corrugated cardboard filled with paraffin).

Equipment Needs

1. *Buddy burner.* A tuna can, rolled corrugated cardboard and paraffin wax.
2. *Stove.* A #10 can (1 gallon), tin snips and a punch-type can opener.
3. *Damper.* Aluminum foil or tuna-can lid, wire, small nail, hammer and coat hanger.
4. *Oven.* Three small flat rocks of equal size (approximately ½ inch high), a tuna can or its lid, a 3-pound shortening can (or a can of comparable size) and 1½ to 2 feet of pliable wire. If an oven with a window is desired, turkey oven wrap (cooking bag) and wire will be needed. A tuna can or lid is used to hold the cooking food.

Preparation
Buddy Burner

To make the burner, cut corrugated cardboard (across the corrugation so its holes show) into strips the same width as the height of the tuna can. Roll the cardboard and place it in the can (Figure 7-3), then pour melted wax over the cardboard. Heat the wax in a double boiler, because if it is overheated, it will burst into flames. Or, set a piece of wax on the cardboard and light a match next to the wax (Figure 7-4). Let the wax melt onto the cardboard, which will catch fire. Continue putting chunks of wax near the flame until the buddy burner is filled with wax.

The cardboard in the buddy burner serves as a wick, and the wax serves as a candle to provide the heat for the stove. A small wick can be placed in the corrugated cardboard for fast and easy lighting. It is also helpful to turn the can on its side so the flame

POPCORN POPPER

Y ou can improvise a sturdy popcorn popper with a large flour sifter and a backpacker rack (or any kind of rack that can be elevated above the coals).

- Pour 2 to 3 tablespoons of popcorn in the flour sifter (Figure 7-5).
- Cover the sifter with foil.
- Place the sifter on the rack, which should be from 3 to 4 inches above the coals, depending upon the intensity of the heat. Shake the sifter back and forth a bit as the popcorn warms to heat it evenly. As the popcorn heats, it will pop and fill the sifter (Figure 7-6). Wear heat-proof gloves to prevent a burn.

Oil is not necessary in this method. The reason oil is used in popping corn in a pan is that the oil helps to heat the corn to the point of popping. With this flour-sifter method, the heat from the coals is sufficient to cause the corn to pop.

Figure 7-5. Pouring popcorn into a flour sifter

Figure 7-6. Sifter filled with popped popcorn

Figure 7-7. Smoke holes in a tin can stove

Figure 7-8. Foil damper

Figure 7-9. Can lid damper

can spread across the cardboard more easily. Filled with wax, the paper will burn for 1½ to 2 hours. To lengthen the buddy burner's heating time, place a chunk of wax on top of the corrugated paper while it is burning. The burner can be used for an indefinite period of time if it is replenished with wax, because the wax burns at a lower temperature than the cardboard, lengthening the life of the cardboard.

Stove

First, cut out one end of the #10 can. Then cut a door about 3 inches high and 4 inches wide on one side of the can at the open end, leaving the top of the door attached. Pull the door open. With a punch-type can opener, punch three to four holes on the backside of the can. These holes will act as a chimney, letting the smoke come out during the cooking process (Figure 7-7).

Damper

You'll need a cover damper to control the heat on the buddy burner. This can be made out of foil or the lid of a can.

If you're using foil, you'll need to fold a length about 1½ times the diameter of the buddy burner. Use three or four thicknesses. Fold one end of the foil back a little more than the diameter of the can. This end will be placed on the can and adjusted back and forth to control the heat (Figure 7-8 on page 87). The other end of the foil is bent at a 90° angle toward the ground to the height of the buddy burner. This end supports the damper and is used to adjust it. To make a damper, use a tuna can lid. Make a wire handle using a coat hanger, preferably a pant hanger that has rolled cardboard around the bottom wire. Attach it to the lid. Remove the cardboard. Bend the two sides together. Make holes in the end of the lid and hook the two ends of the hanger to it with wire. Bend the end of the handle at a 90° angle so it forms a support to hold the end of the can flat to the buddy burner. The damper can be pulled forward and backward to control the heat (Figure 7-9 on page 87).

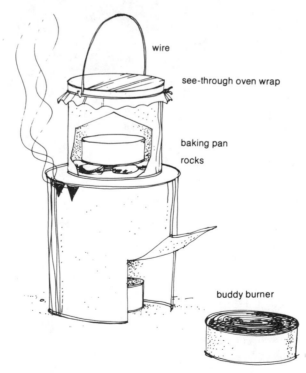

Figure 7-10. Buddy burner in a tin-can-stove oven

Oven

To use this simple oven, place the food in a tuna can or on its lid. Set it on the stove, and then place the oven — made from a coffee can or a foil dome — over them to bake.

To make a coffee can oven, cut both ends out of a can and wire transparent oven wrap tightly over one end so the food inside will be visible (Figure 7-10). Make a handle by hooking the end of a wire through a hole punched on each side of the can. If a coffee can is not available, shape aluminum foil into a dome that will fit over the top of the stove.

Billy Can

A homemade oven, called a billy can, can be made easily from a #10 can and a hanger or a heavy wire. Cut one end out of the can and punch two small holes on opposite sides of that end for the handle. Be sure to bend back the metal in the punched holes so there will be no rough edges that might cut someone. Straighten out a coat hanger or wire, then curve it, securing the two ends to the holes punched through the can (Figure 7-11).

Foods

Small amounts of food that can be cooked in a frying pan are great for cooking on top of the tin can stove. Eggs in a basket, bacon, hamburgers and tacos are a few of the foods that can be prepared using the stove as a frying pan. When the stove is made into an oven, it can be used to bake miniature cakes, pies and cookies.

Figure 7-11.
Billy can

Steps

Frying

- Light the buddy burner and place it under the can.
- Place the damper over the buddy burner to control the amount of heat. The can stove will be ready to use in seconds.

Boiling

- Place food to be boiled in a can on the stove top.
- Light the burner and slide it under the stove. The liquid will soon be boiling. If this is too slow, cut the top off the #10 can and soap the outside bottom of a frying pan.
- Place the frying pan on top of the can and cook.

This is excellent for emergency cooking; however, only use this method of cooking outdoors.

Baking

- Place food on a tuna-can lid or, if it is cake batter, pour it into a clean, greased tuna can. If you think the food might stick to the tuna can, insert a folded 1-inch strip of aluminum foil, folding it over the edge of the can and down across the inside, leaving enough foil over both edges to pull upward after the food has been cooked. The food will then come out of the can easily.
- Place three rocks ½-inch high in a triangular shape on the tin can stove.
- Place the tuna lid or can of batter on the rocks, which will hold the food above the stove and prevent the bottom from burning by allowing the air circulating around the oven to bake the food.
- Cover the food with the shortening can and let it bake.

A good item to bake in the tin-can-stove oven is a pineapple up-side-down cake. Grease the inside of the tuna can, then place the 1-inch strip of aluminum foil in the can. Place one slice of pineapple in the can with a maraschino cherry in its center. Sprinkle 1 tablespoon of brown sugar over the pineapple and pour about 1 tablespoon of pineapple juice over that. Fill the can about two-thirds full of cake batter, then place it in the oven of the tin can stove. It will take about 20 minutes for the cake to bake.

EARMUFF TOAST

Bread purchased at the grocery store can be toasted on the side of a warm #10 can. On a cold morning, your hands will be warmed as you hold the toast to the side of the can.

- Take two slices of bread, and place them on opposite sides of the warm can, just behind the oven door. Roll the bread on with your hands.
- After you have held the bread for a moment, it will usually stick to the outside of the can.
- With a spatula or a knife, pop the bread off when it has browned. Toast only one side of the bread because the toast takes on the shape of the can.

Tall Can Stove

The tall can stove is a quick method for cooking meats that have only a small amount of fat.

Principle

Dry heat given off by flaming newspapers cooks the meat on the rack in the stove. Juice from the meat drips down on the papers and keeps them burning. This method is much like barbecuing meats. Foods cooked this way will have a definite smoky flavor.

Fire(s)

The fuel for this method of cooking is rolled-up newspapers. Four or five sheets of newspaper are loosely twisted and crushed lightly into small "logs," then placed in the stove bottom. A single sheet of newspaper wadded and set on top of the logs is lighted first. The fats dripping from the meat will keep the log papers burning. Do not use sections with colored ink. They may produce toxic fumes when burned.

Equipment Needs

The items you will need to make a tall can stove include: a square 5-gallon can, a can opener, a wire rack that fits on the can (do not use refrigerator racks; some give off toxic fumes), newspapers, and a water spray bottle or water pistol.

Preparation

To build the stove, remove the top from a large can, such as a 5-gallon honey can. You may need a knife and a hammer to cut around the corners. Cut one 2½-inch vent on one side of the can about 3 inches from the bottom. Place a cookie cooling rack over the top of the can for the grill. Meat that is not more than 1 inch thick and has some fat is best cooked on this stove.

Steps

- After the bottom of the can is filled with twisted rolls of newspaper, lightly crumple about a half sheet of single newspaper and place it on top of the rolled paper (Figure 7-12).
- When the stove is ready for cooking, set a match to the single sheet.
- Place the rack of meat on the stove (Figure 7-13).
- If the flames become too high, spray them with water from a spray bottle or a water pistol.
- If not enough fat drips from the meat to keep the flames burning, place 2-inch strips of bacon or fat between the meat until the flames flare up.

Recipes for Contact Heat

Ways of cooking in the open with contact heat are almost endless, and so are recipes. Some of these recipes are old favorites with a new twist or two for more lip-smacking goodness.

ORANGE, EGG AND MUFFIN BREAKFAST

Method: *Contact heat*
Time: *15 to 20 minutes*

- Cut in half and carefully remove
  fruit from both halves of   1 orange
- Break into one half of the cup-
  shaped orange peel   1 egg
- In the other half, place   batter for 1 muffin

Place each half-orange on foil large enough to bring to the top and twist. Place the foil-wrapped orange in hot coals for the required 15 to 20 minutes. Serves 1.

Figure 7-12. Newspaper crumpled in a tall can stove

Figure 7-13. Steak on a tall can stove

HUSH PUPPIES

Method: *Dutch oven*
Time: *1 to 2 minutes on each side*

- Sift together
- Add
- Stir and add

Sift together	1 cup cornmeal
	1 tablespoon flour
	1 teaspoon baking powder
	1 teaspoon salt
Add	¼ cup finely diced onion
	½ chopped green pepper
Stir and add	1 egg, well beaten
	⅓ cup milk

Form little balls with this batter and drop them into hot oil. The batter will bubble when put in oil. Keep turning them until brown. Remove the hush puppies and drain on paper towels. Serves 4.

TV DINNER

Method: *Wet newspapers and foil*
Time: *20 to 35 minutes*

When coals are hot, wet two layers of	newspaper
Center on the long side of the wet newspaper	1 TV dinner

Fold newspaper over top and roll. Then wrap in foil. Place on coals and put coals on top. Cook the recommended time as if you were cooking at home. Serves 1.

MIXED-VEGETABLE FOIL DINNER

Method: *Foil cooking*
Time: *10 to 15 minutes per side*

On one piece of heavy-duty foil place	1 to 2 slices of a large onion
Shape a patty from	¼ pound hamburger
With the patty, place on a piece of foil	1 teaspoon dry gravy mix, seasoned salt and pepper
	⅓ cup canned mixed vegetables
	⅓ cup canned, sliced white potatoes

- Optional

    1 teaspoon dry gravy mix
        over top
    1 slice of large onion

Wrap in foil, using drugstore wrap method (see page 113), and cook on coals or grill 10 to 15 minutes per side. Serves 1.

ROASTED CORN

Method: *Contact heat*
Time: *15 to 20 minutes*
- Carefully pull back husk and remove
  silk of

    1 ear of corn
- While corn is still wet, sprinkle
  lightly with

    salt

Replace husk so no corn is exposed and place it on a hot bed of coals, turning it one-fourth the way around every 3 to 5 minutes (corn can also be wrapped in foil). Remove the husk, butter the corn and eat it immediately.

To roast corn faster, simply toss fresh-picked corn (in the husk) onto the coals and rotate so that it cooks evenly, approximately 5 minutes per side.

Remove from coals and open to remove silk. Butter and salt it to taste. Serves 1.

PUFFED POTATOES

Method: *Skillet or Dutch oven*
Time: *15 to 20 minutes*
- Mix together

    1 cup mashed potatoes (may
        substitute rehydrated
        potatoes)
    1 cup flour
    ⅓ cup milk
    2 teaspoons baking powder
    1 teaspoon salt
- Drop mixture by spoonfuls into

    hot grease (2 inches deep)

Brown on both sides. Makes 15 to 20 small puffs. Serves 2 to 3.

QUICK SCONES

Method: *Dutch oven or frying pan*
Time: *3 to 5 minutes*

- Place in pan to heat   ½ pound (2 cups) shortening
                                          or oil

- Cut in half (or in quarters)   4 English muffins
- With a fork, dip muffin into   basic pancake batter

Drop bread into hot oil. Turn when they are golden brown and brown on the other side.

Serve plain or roll scones in sugar and cinnamon or powdered sugar, or spread with honey, jam, jelly or syrup. Serves 2.

BRIGHTEN-UP BREAKFAST

Method: *Dutch oven or frying pan*
Time: **Method 1** — 10 to 15 minutes; **Method 2** — 20 minutes, if potatoes are cooked

Preparation Method 1 (fast and easy):
- Slice in small pieces and fry   ½ pound bacon
- Drain away most of the bacon
  grease. Cube and add   1 can potatoes (29 ounces)
- Salt and pepper potatoes to taste.
- Scramble and fry in separate pan   6 eggs
- Add eggs to mixture.
- Season as desired.

Preparation Method 2:
- Boil, peel and cube   4 medium potatoes
- Slice in pieces and fry   ½ pound bacon
- Drain off most of the grease.
- Add cubed potatoes and salt and
  pepper to taste.
- Fry until potatoes are browned.
- Add and scramble together   6 eggs

Add more salt and pepper if necessary. When eggs are cooked, serve plain or with catsup. Serves 3 to 4.

Note: Diced ham or Spam can be substituted for bacon.

Roughing It Easy

SHEEPHERDER'S STEW

Method: *Dutch oven*
Time: *35 minutes*

- Brown

  1 pound ground beef
  ½ teaspoon salt
  4 diced raw potatoes
  carrots (2 to 3 peeled and
      diced)
  ½ diced onion

- Add

  2 cans cream of mushroom
      soup
  ½ soup can milk

Cook over low heat until vegetables and meat are tender (25 minutes).

- If desired, drain and add

  1 can green beans
  1 can liquid-packed corn

Cook an additional 10 minutes to heat vegetables. Serves 6 to 8.

STUFFED GREEN PEPPERS

Method: *Foil cooking*
Time: *30 minutes*

- Mix together

  ½ pound hamburger
  salt and pepper to taste
  1 egg
  ¼ diced onion

- Stuff mixture into

  4 green peppers, scraped out

Place peppers on individual pieces of foil and wrap using the drugstore wrap technique (see page 113). Place over coals and cook 12 to 15 minutes on each side. Serves 2.

FOIL HAM AND CHEESE ROLLS

Method: *Foil cooking*
Time: *10 to 15 minutes*

- Make two cuts 1 inch apart across
  the top of

  hard dinner rolls

- Mix together the following

  1 can deviled ham
  ¼ cup diced sweet pickles
  ⅛ teaspoon garlic salt

- Spread this mixture generously inside each cut.
- Insert inside each cut   1 piece of cheese
- Sprinkle top with   Parmesan cheese

Wrap each in foil and place in coals for 10 minutes or until warmed through. Serves 1.

FRUIT FRITTERS

Method: *Skillet or tin can stove*
Time: *10 to 20 minutes*

- Make a batter with

  1 egg
  1 teaspoon baking powder
  ¾ cup flour
  ¼ teaspoon salt
  ½ cup milk

- Pour oil into frying pan until it is 1 inch deep and heat.
- Dip into batter and fry until golden brown either of the following sliced: apples

  bananas

Roll in powdered sugar. Use as appetizers or snacks. Serves 1.

MEXICALI SALLY ("EAT-WITH-A-FORK TACOS")

Method: *Skillet*
Time: *15 minutes*

- Fry in a large skillet   1 pound ground beef

  ½ onion, chopped

- Drain grease and add   large can of chili beans (30 ounces)

- Continue cooking until well heated.
- Slice in small pieces and do not combine   ½ head of lettuce

  3 tomatoes

- Grate   ½ pound of cheese
- Place on plate   1 handful of tortilla chips
- Serve with   1 can taco sauce

Serve on plate in the following order: tortilla chips, meat and beans, lettuce, cheese, taco sauce. Serves 4.

CHICKEN WITH RICE

Method: *Dutch oven*

Time: *About 45 minutes*

- In oiled Dutch oven, brown   1 chicken, cut into pieces
- Sprinkle with   salt and pepper
- Combine   2 10½-ounce cans of cream of chicken soup

                                             1 cup instant rice

- And spoon over chicken.
- Sprinkle with   ½ cup Parmesan cheese

Place Dutch oven on coals and cover lid with coals. Bake 35-45 minutes. Serves 4.

Novelty Cooking Methods

Outdoor cooking has its share of novelty cooking methods. The possibilities are limited only by your imagination. One of the most exciting things that can happen in outdoor cooking is the creation of new, unique methods for cooking food. After trying the following ideas, stretch your imagination and develop some of your own methods.

Cooking Directly on Coals

The direct heat of the coals cooks food without any other equipment. It is best to use hardwood coals if there is to be direct contact with the food.

Some foods are very tasty cooked directly on hot coals. The following are only a few suggestions:

- **Toast.** Place a slice of bread directly on white glowing coals. Turn the bread over after about a minute. Before buttering the toast, blow and brush away the white ashes. Bread can be placed between folded foil and toasted in the same way.
- **Ash cakes.** From a stiff biscuit dough, make small flat cakes and place them on a bed of white ashes. Turn them when they are golden brown. A little brown sugar or jam in the center of two thin ash cakes makes a good pastry.

TURNOVERS

Delicious turnovers can be made with English muffins:

- Scrape out the center of both sides of an English muffin with a fork or spoon, taking care not to scrape a hole in the bun (Figure 7-14).
- Fill one half of the muffin with your favorite sandwich or dessert filling (Figure 7-15).

Suggestions:

- Sandwich:

  egg salad
  cheese
  ham and cheese
  deviled ham with pickles
  diced Spam with pickles and salad
    dressing
- Dessert:

  cherry
  peach
  apple
  other (try your own)

- Cover the filled half of the muffin with the other half and butter both on the outside.
- Wrap the muffin with foil, using the drugstore wrap technique on page 113.
- Place it in coals for 3 to 5 minutes per side. Serves 1.

Figure 7-14. Scraping the center out of a muffin

Figure 7-15. Filling half of a muffin with cherry pie filling

- **Meats.** If there is no other way to cook fish, steak or hot dogs, place them over hot coals and cook. Fish should be cooked in the skin.

Rock Cooking

Method 1

Heat can be conducted through a rock from coals or fire below. Find a flat rock that is not over 2 inches thick. Rocks that have recently been in water or that retain moisture, such as shell and limestone, should be avoided because they may explode when heated. Make a keyhole fire, brace the clean rock over the square part of the keyhole, and put hot coals under it. Heat the rock slowly. If one side heats too fast and expands more quickly than the other side, the rock may break. Turn the rock over and allow it to heat on the other side gradually and as evenly as possible.

When the rock is hot, it can be placed directly over the coals and used as a grill. When the upper surface cools, turn the rock over, brush it off, and cook on the hot side. If a rock is thin enough, the heat will be conducted through it and it will not need to be turned. The food may be cooked directly on the hot surface of the rock, or the rock may be covered with foil.

Method 2

Food may also be cooked on a round, hot rock with a smooth, flat side. It should be neither too large nor too thick and should be hard enough that it won't break or explode when heated. Heat the rock in the fire, turning it occasionally to permit it to heat evenly. Remove it when it is hot and brush the ashes away before cooking on it. Use the rock for cooking foods that can be fried quickly. (See Figure 7-16 on page 102.) When the rock cools, return it to the fire to reheat it.

Method 3 (Backpacker's Chicken)

A chicken can be prepared at breakfast, then wrapped in foil and newspaper and placed in your backpack for 3 hours, and finally eaten at lunch (Figure 7-17). As unbelievable as it sounds, it really works. The newspaper insulates the chicken, allowing it to continue cooking.

You must first find a rock that will fill the cavity of the chicken. Then find two rocks approximately the size of your clenched fist, which will go under each wing. Place the rocks in

Figure 7-16. Bacon cooking on a heated rock

Figure 7-17. Backpacker's chicken

hot rocks

Figure 7-18. Cooking food on the manifold of a car

the fire while you are cooking breakfast. The rocks should be in the fire for 60 minutes or until they are extremely hot.

Make a 1-inch stack of opened newspapers, and place a 2-foot piece of 18-inch wide heavy-duty foil on top of the stack. Place the chicken on top of the foil. Wearing gloves, take a pair of tongs and remove the rocks from the fire. Wrap them in foil, taking special care not to burn yourself in the process. Then using the tongs, put the larger rock in the cavity of the chicken and the two smaller rocks under each wing. Pour barbecue sauce over the chicken.

Bring the foil together and roll it down in small folds following the drugstore wrap technique (see page 113). Fold the foil in on the ends. Now bring the bundle over to one side of the newspaper and wrap the package in ¼-inch stack of newspapers. Continue this until you have used the whole stack of papers. Place the package into a backpack and take it on your hike. After 3 hours, open up the package; you will have the most delicious barbecued chicken.

Manifold of a Car

Creativity is really what this book is all about, and a creative way to cook while you travel is to use the manifold of your car. This is possible if you can find a flat area on the manifold so the food will not slip off. The food is cooked by heat from the pipe that carries hot air into the exhaust.

Place the food on a piece of foil and wrap it using the drugstore wrap technique. Wrap the foil package in a second piece of foil, also sealing it tightly to protect against juice leakage.

To find the manifold, look under the car and locate the exhaust. Follow it up into the engine; the point where the pipe leads into the engine is the manifold. If you can secure a foil package on your car, you can cook while traveling.

Once you've secured the foil package onto the manifold of your car, begin driving (Figure 7-18). The food will cook about as fast as it would at the medium temperature in a range oven, but you will have to watch it carefully the first time because the amount of heat will differ from car to car. When the food is about half cooked, stop and turn it over. This can add wonderful adventure to any trip.

Cooking Hamburger on a Shovel

If you need an extra frying pan for cooking hamburgers, a large shovel with a long handle will work well. Clean off the shovel as well as you can, then cover the shovel with two layers of heavy-duty aluminum foil. Place the shovel on a bed of hot coals to warm it. Then place the hamburger on the shovel and cook. If you don't want to sit down and hold the shovel, find a rock to prop the handle up.

When the hamburgers are ready, you can sit on your log and use the long handle of the shovel to serve the hamburgers to everyone around the campfire.

Nonutensil Cookery

Nonutensil cookery consists of some of the most unique cooking methods and is fun to experiment with.

Cooking Food Inside of Food

A novel way to prepare some items of food is to cook them inside of other foods. The outside foods act as natural buffers against the heat while giving the foods inside additional flavor.

Cooking Inside an Orange

When cooking inside an orange, use an orange with a thick skin because it's easier to remove the meat from the orange. To prepare the orange, cut it in half and place your fingers between the meat of the orange and the skin. Slide your fingers back and forth to loosen and separate the meat from the skin. A spoon can also be used to remove the meat of the orange. Eggs, muffins or cakes cook well in the shell. With cakes and muffins, fill the shell two-thirds full of batter. Place the shell on a square piece of heavy-duty foil, bringing the foil up around the orange and coming together at the top of the orange. Leave enough room for the food to rise in the shell. Place it on the hot coals for 10 minutes or until the food is cooked. Gingerbread or chocolate cake are fun to make this way.

Cooking Inside an Onion

Cooking hamburger or other items that can be flavored by onions is quick and easy using this method. Take a large onion and peel off the outer, non-edible layer. Cut the onion in half and pop out the centers, saving the centers for cooking later. If you have trouble removing the center where the root is, cut off the root. Place the food to be cooked in the center of the onion halves. Wrap each half in foil and place them on a bed of coals to cook. The cooking time will vary depending on what you are cooking; for example, an egg placed in one half of an onion and wrapped in foil will take 15 minutes to cook. Hamburger takes 15 minutes on each side.

Marshmallows and Chocolate Inside Banana (Banana Boat)

Cut a wedge-shaped section out of the length of a banana. Place marshmallows and chocolate chips or pieces of chocolate bars into the cavity of the banana. Wrap the banana boat in foil and heat for 4 to 6 minutes. Other foods that can be placed in the banana boat are pineapple, maraschino cherries and nuts.

Boiling Water in a Paper Cup

When liquid is heated in a paper cup, the container will not burn. This means water or milk can be heated in an unwaxed paper cup placed in the coals. (See Figure 7-19 on page 106.) If the flame touches the top of the cup where there is no liquid, the cup can burn. Eggs can also be hard cooked in this manner. Milk can be heated in its carton if there is no wax on it.

Breakfast in a Paper Bag

Use a lunch-sized paper bag on the end of a pointed stick to cook your bacon and eggs for breakfast. Cut a strip of bacon in half and cover the bottom of the paper bag with it. Break an egg into the sack over the bacon. Roll the top of the sack halfway down in 1-inch folds and push a stick through the roll at the top of the bag. Hold the bag over the coals. Grease will coat the bottom of the bag as it cooks. The egg will cook in about 10 minutes. (See Figure 7-20 on page 106.) (You can also cook the bacon and eggs by setting the bag on a piece of foil.) Be careful. If the sack gets too near the coals, it will burn. When the eggs and bacon are done, roll down the sides of the sack and eat your breakfast.

Can Barbecue

The can barbecue is a simple method of cooking outdoors by placing charcoal briquets in a can.

Figure 7-19.
Water heating in
a paper cup over
coals

Figure 7-20. Eggs and bacon cooking over coals in a paper bag

Roughing It Easy

Principle

Use the outdoor can barbecue for stick, spit, aluminum foil and grill cooking. The food is cooked by dry heat given off by coals or by charcoal briquets. The food will have a smoked flavor if wood briquets are used.

Fire(s)

Charcoal briquets or coals are used for preparing food with this method. See pages 64-66 for ways of preparing briquets for use. Crisscross or log-cabin fires will produce coals quickly.

Equipment Needs

The equipment you will need includes: 1-gallon can, aluminum foil, wire rack and tin snips; or a #10 can, punch-type can opener, can opener, wire grill and stick or hanger.

Preparation

There are two major kinds of can barbecues: (1) a 5-gallon can (such as a honey can) cut in half lengthwise and its sharp edges hammered down, and (2) a #10 can. To prepare, follow these suggestions:

- Place bricks under the can if it is resting on a cement surface.
- Line the container with 2 inches of gravel, dirt or sand so the coals won't heat the metal.
- Pile the charcoal briquets on the gravel, dirt or sand and light them, using one of the methods suggested in chapter five on fire building.
- Before you begin to cook, spread the briquets evenly over the prepared area.

One way to prepare a #10-can barbecue is to cut eight vertical lines one-third of the way down the sides of the can and bend back the metal strips to form a fan shape. (See Figures 7-21, 7-22 and 7-23 on page 108.) Line the can with aluminum foil and add the charcoal briquets, covering them with a wire rack. Prop the can up a little so the briquets get oxygen.

Another way to prepare a can barbecue is to cut both ends out of a can and place hot coals or briquets inside it. The food may be cooked on a rack on top of the can or with sticks or hangers.

Figure 7-21. #10 can barbecue

Figure 7-22. Can barbecue lined with foil

Figure 7-23. Place the grill over the foil

Foods

Foods that can be cooked on a stick or spit or over coals can be cooked in a can barbecue. Foods that are oven-broiled can be barbecued, using the equipment described.

Steps

See the sections on stick, spit and aluminum foil for both equipment and steps to follow. For grilling, a wire rack and rocks or bricks will be necessary to hold the grill above the coals.

Pit Cooking

Although it takes time and effort to dig the pit and prepare the coals and ingredients for pit cooking, after the food has been placed in the pit, the hard work is done. Food wrapped in foil or leaves or placed in a Dutch oven cooks well in a pit. This is one of the few outdoor methods good for cooking large items such as whole chickens, hams, turkeys or roasts. By layering foods in the pit—meats, then potatoes, then vegetables, then even desserts—a whole meal can be cooked underground.

Principle

Heat is retained in the rocks and coals buried in the ground just as heat is retained in an oven at home. The main difference is the variation of heat. The pit starts very hot and gradually cools, while a commercial oven has a constant heat. Foods can be cooked to perfection in a pit even with this variance in heat.

Fire(s)

Build a crisscross fire that will produce many coals. Burn logs 2 to 4 inches in diameter. Unless you want an extremely hot pit for cooking a turkey or a pig, logs larger than 4 inches in diameter will take too long to burn down. Add logs to the fire as it burns; many coals are necessary. It takes about 1 hour to heat the rocks and to fill the pit with coals and ashes.

Equipment Needs

All that is needed to prepare for cooking in a pit is a long-handled shovel and some flat rocks. Do not use rocks that retain moisture,

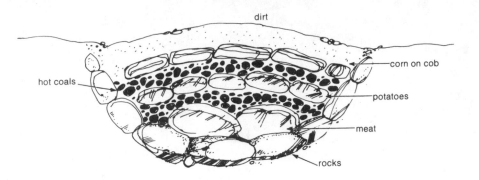

Figure 7-24. Underground pit cooking

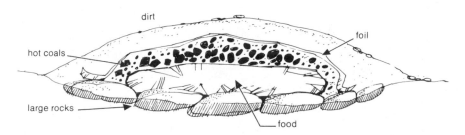

Figure 7-25. Aboveground pit cooking

such as rocks from stream beds or limestone or sandstone, because they may explode.

Preparation
Underground Pit

- Dig a hole two to three times larger than the Dutch oven or the total size of the foil packages that will go into the pit (Figure 7-24). Remember that there should be room for rocks and smaller packages of food should have 2 or 3 inches of coal between each of them.
- Line the pit with flat rocks.
- Build a fire in the pit and let it burn rapidly for at least an hour. When the pit is almost filled with coals, it is ready for food to be placed in it.

Aboveground Pit
If digging is not permitted or if the ground is too moist, prepare an aboveground pit by laying a base of flat rocks and surrounding

that base with larger rocks (Figure 7-25). After building the fire and forming a large bed of hot coals, remove the coals, place the food on the rocks, and cover it with the coals. Cover the food and coals with foil, and place about 3 inches of dirt over the entire pit.

Foods

This is an excellent method for cooking complete meals, including roast, ham or poultry; potatoes, corn on the cob and other vegetables; and desserts that can be cooked in a Dutch oven or wrapped in foil.

Chickens or turkeys can be stuffed if desired. So flavors can cook through, meats should be seasoned before being wrapped in foil. Many packages of chicken or other meats can be cooked in the same pit.

Steps

- Prepare foods for the pit while the fire is burning down by wrapping them 2 times in heavy-duty foil. The drugstore wrap technique should be used for sealing food.
- Remove the hot coals from the center of the pit and place them to the side of the pit. Don't spread the coals out any more than necessary because you will waste some of the heat.
- Place each wrapped item in the pit according to the length of time it requires for cooking. Each item needs to be *completely* covered with coals. Two packages that touch each other won't cook well. Items requiring a longer time for cooking should be placed near the bottom of the pit, whereas those requiring a shorter cooking time will cook more slowly near the top surface of the pit. A thin layer of dirt can be shoveled over the coals between two items of food to cut down the heat. It will take practice to cook well this way because temperatures and times vary depending upon the type of wood used and the number of coals you have.
- Place a section of newspaper over the coals before covering. When you dig up the pit later on, the newspaper will indicate that you are getting closer to the food.
- Cover coals in the pit with 4 to 6 inches of dirt. To make the coals steam, put wet burlap over the pit before covering the

coals with dirt. Also, a fire built over the pit will increase the temperature inside the pit.

- Allow meat about the size of a chicken to cook from 3 to 3½ hours. Subtract or add time to this amount for smaller or larger items. Cut a large roast into smaller pieces to reduce cooking time.
- When the allotted time is up, carefully remove the food from the pit with a shovel. Be careful not to pierce or cut into the food packages. You will need gloves to remove the packages because they will be hot. For easy removal of large foil packages, wrap them with wire long enough to protrude from the top of the pit. This will allow you to locate the packages when they are done and will prevent breaking the foil with the shovel.

Aluminum Foil Cookery

Cooking in aluminum foil is the modern version of cooking food in leaves and clay. It is clean and easy, and there are no pots to carry or dishes to wash.

Principle
Aluminum foil is used to broil, braise, fry, sauté and steam foods. Steaming, the most common method, is done by sealing the food in foil so moisture cannot escape.

Fire(s)
A fire that can rapidly produce a 2-inch bed of coals is necessary for foil cooking. A crisscross or log-cabin fire is best, but charcoal briquets are also good. When wood is at a premium or so soft that it burns too fast, use a combination of wood and briquets. (See chapter five on fire building.)

Equipment Needs
The basic equipment is aluminum foil, which can be purchased in regular and heavy-duty weights. The heavy-duty weight is more desirable because of its additional strength.

Preparation
To make a foil pan, cut a green willow switch flexible enough to make a loop at the end about the size of a frying pan. Secure

DRUGSTORE WRAP

- Cut two pieces of lightweight foil or one piece of heavy-duty foil twice the circumference of the item to be wrapped.
- Place the food in the middle of the shiny side of one piece of foil (Figure 7-26).
- Bring the opposite sides of the foil together, and fold it ½ inch at a time, turning it down in small folds until it can be folded no longer (Figure 7-27).
- Flatten the top of the package, then roll the open edges toward the center in small folds (Figures 7-28 and 7-29). The edges of the package must be tightly sealed.
- If the package needs to be wrapped again, place the folded top of the package downward in the center of the other piece of foil and fold.

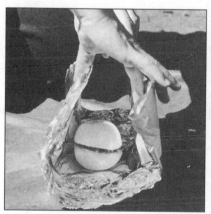

Figure 7-26. Place the food in the foil

Figure 7-27. Fold the ends of the foil

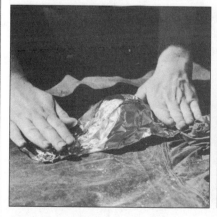

Figure 7-28. Flatten the folded foil

Figure 7-29. Roll the ends of the foil

the loop to the stick with wire or by tying it (Figure 7-30 and 7-32). If a loop cannot be made, cut a forked stick (Figure 7-31); cut off the forked ends evenly about 4 to 8 inches beyond the forked joint, depending upon the size of pan desired. Whether you use the loop or the fork, cut a piece of foil that extends 3 inches beyond the size of the loop or the fork. If you desire the pan to have depth, allow the foil to sag in the middle. After forming the pan, roll the excess foil as far under and around the stick as possible.

A frying pan can also be made from a coat hanger by straightening the hook and pulling the center bottom wire to form a square. Place foil across the wire and wrap it around twice. To make a handle, tightly wire the straightened hook to a stick so it will not turn.

Foods
Foods such as meats, vegetables and fruits are those most commonly cooked with foil; steaming is the most common method used. Entire dinners are often put together and cooked in one piece of foil. Foil cooking can be useful in many other ways:

- Warming bread
- Cooking vegetables (corn on the cob, etc.)
- Frying bacon and eggs
- Boiling small amounts of water or other liquids.

Steps

- Cut two pieces of lightweight foil or one piece of heavy-duty foil twice the circumference of the item to be wrapped.
- Place the food in the middle of one piece of foil.
- Add a little water if there is not much moisture in the food.
- Bring the opposite sides of the foil together, then follow the drugstore wrap technique.
- If the package needs to be wrapped again, place the folded top of the package downward in the center of the other piece of foil. See page 113 for complete instructions.

Wrap the second piece of foil exactly like the first, but if heavy-duty foil is used, one layer is usually enough.

If the coals are very hot or if you are using briquets, you can

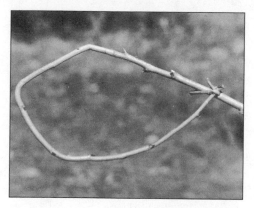

Figure 7-30. Branch frame for foil frying pan

Figure 7-31. Fish in a forked-stick frying pan

Figure 7-32. Hamburger in a foil frying pan

prevent the food from overcooking by rolling the first package of foil in three layers of newspaper before wrapping it in the second layer of foil. Another way to prevent overcooking is to place vegetables that have a high moisture content around the food. For example: Place sliced onions on both sides of a hamburger dinner; wrap a meat loaf in cabbage leaves; place tomato slices in a foil dinner. A third way to make sure your dinner doesn't burn is to turn the dinner every 5 minutes while it is on the coals to prevent one spot from getting too hot.

CHAPTER 8

Enclosed and Concentrated Heat — Your Camping Oven

An oven can be created by enclosing heat and letting the air circulate. Some materials used to enclose heat are foil, cans, a cardboard box lined with foil and a Dutch oven. The reflector oven is an exception to this. Food is placed on the reflector oven rack and close enough to the flames that the concentrated heat cooks the food.

Creative Oven Ideas

Pie Tin Oven

Two pie tins can be used to make an oven that will bake biscuits, pie, cake, pizza and other foods.

- Oil one pie tin and place food in it.
- Turn a second pie tin upside down over the first tin to make a lid.
- Use three or four metal clips (such as Bulldog clips used to clamp paper together) an equal distance apart on the lip of the pans.
- Place three rocks or spikes in a bed of coals high enough to elevate the pie tin oven 1 inch above the coals.
- Place coals on the lid. If more coals are needed than will cover the lid, a collar can be made by folding a length of foil two or three times and hooking it together at the ends. The collar will fit around the pie tin to hold the coals.
- Charcoal briquets get very hot, so place them in a checkerboard pattern, leaving plenty of space between briquets.

Cooking time should be about the same as it would be in a home oven. Either pliers or heat-proof gloves will be needed to remove the clips. Care should be taken to brush the coals off before opening the lid.

Chicken Under Inverted Can

The following cooking method is a basic oven. Many foods can be cooked this way.

- Sharpen one end of a sweet bark stick 14 to 20 inches long and thrust it into the ground to make a hole that will be used later.
- Remove the stick, split the other end and wedge a clean stone between the split ends to hold them approximately 2 or 3 inches apart.
- Sharpen both split ends.
- Insert the split ends of the stick through the opening in the chicken and into its rib cage so the chicken won't slip down on the stick while it is cooking (Figure 8-1).
- Place a piece of foil over the previously made hole; push the end of the stick through the foil.
- Push the end of the stick into the ground so a 5-gallon can (with one end cut out) can be set down over the chicken until the can rests on the ground. (A metal bucket or small metal garbage can can also be used if you are unable to find a 5-gallon can.) The chicken should not touch the sides of the can or it will burn.
- Place hot coals or charcoal briquets on top of, around the bottom and stacked up the sides of the can (Figure 8-2).

Hardwood coals are needed to keep the temperature up. The cooking time will vary from 90 to 120 minutes, depending on how brown you want the chicken. So that you will not "pepper" the chicken with ashes when you remove the can, brush the coals from the top first. Charcoal briquets are an excellent heat source. Check them after 30 minutes to evaluate the temperature of the oven.

Inverted Dutch Oven and Frying Pan

Fried foods can be cooked on the inverted lid of a Dutch oven at the same time that a delicious pie is cooking for lunch or dinner.

Figure 8-1. Chicken covered with a 5-gallon can

Figure 8-2. Can covered with hot coals

To master this simple time-saving method, dig a small hole about 9 to 12 inches in diameter by 3 to 4 inches deep. Place coals about ¾ of an inch high in the hole and place the rack on the ground. The rack should be 2 to 3 inches above the coals. Place the pie on the rack (other foods to be cooked can be placed in the pan), and turn a 12-inch Dutch oven with legs upside down over it. The Dutch oven shouldn't touch the sides of the pan. Spread coals over the bottom of the Dutch oven. Place the Dutch oven lid upside down on the legs of the oven so you'll have a surface to cook on. Let the lid warm for a few minutes, then place the food to be cooked on the lid. The pie should take approximately the same amount of time to cook as it would in your oven at home. Steak, eggs, bacon, hamburger or anything that cooks in a frying pan may be cooked on the lid.

Inverted Lid Oven

An oven can be constructed by using a large lid from a roasting pan or large container. A rack with legs, such as a backpacker's rack or a large wire grill, is placed above the coals. Make a small pan by using heavy-duty foil 2 inches smaller than the circumference of the lid. Place the lid over the foil, and let the hot air circulate around the edges to bake the food. To regulate the heat, raise and lower the rack.

An aluminum dishpan with an empty thread spool bolted to it to serve as a handle may also be used as an oven (Figure 8-3). To attach the spool to the pan, make a hole in the center of the pan large enough for a ⅛-inch bolt 3 inches long. Place a washer on top of the spool and one inside next to the lid, before tightening the nut.

Muffin Pan Oven

Two muffin pans make a very serviceable outdoor oven.

- Line the compartments of a muffin pan with cupcake liners. If liners are not available, oil the compartments (Figure 8-4).
- Fill the compartments with different foods, including hamburger, vegetables and muffin or cake batter (Figure 8-5).
- Season the foods.
- For easy cleaning of the top pan, place a liner over the foods that might stick.
- Fit the second muffin pan over the first.
- Clamp the muffin pans together with four large clips, the kind used to clip paper together (Figure 8-6).
- Keeping the muffin pans level, place them on four rocks over medium-hot coals and put hot coals on top of the "oven," making sure that more coals cover the meat end than the dough end.
- Cook for 25 to 35 minutes.

Reflector Oven

Campers who roast or bake foods in a reflector oven are in for a real treat. This is one of the few methods of outdoor cooking in which the cook can watch the cooking process.

Figure 8-3. Pizza in an inverted dishpan

Figure 8-4. Muffin pans lined to keep food from sticking

Figure 8-5. Muffin pan filled with food

Figure 8-6. Clamped muffin pans with coals covering the top

Principle

A reflector oven operates with a concentration of dry heat. This outdoor method closely duplicates the process of the oven in your home: dry heat is created, then reflected from the walls of your oven around the food. Similarly, heat from the open fire is reflected off foil, metal or rock into the oven and from the sides of the reflector oven (Figure 8-7).

Figure 8-7. Reflector oven

Fire(s)

The best type of fire for the reflector oven is a tepee fire. If the wind is blowing, or if you do not have a fire with good flames, build a fire reflector on the side of the fire opposite the reflector oven. This will help reflect the heat from the fire back into the oven. A fire or heat reflector can be built in any of the following ways:

- Build the fire close to a rock. The rock will reflect heat into the reflector oven.

- Stack up a wall of rocks to reflect the heat. The wall may need to be braced from behind by a heavy log.
- If two reflector ovens are available, place them across the fire from each other so the ovens are facing. This will provide maximum reflection.
- Construct a heat reflector by placing two sticks securely in the ground side by side and stretching foil between them.

Equipment Needs

- **Cookie sheet reflector oven:** Five straight cookie sheets, metal rings, small bolts or wires.
- **Sheet metal reflector oven:** Sheet metal; metal rings; aluminum foil; green sticks; stiff, heavy wire.

A reflector oven may be purchased, or it can be constructed at home or at the campsite itself. The purchased ovens usually fold up and transport easily, and some home-constructed reflector ovens can be made to collapse.

Preparation

There are a variety of ways to construct a reflector oven. Following are some suggestions. Choose the one that best suits your needs and on-hand supplies.

Cookie Sheet Reflector Oven

Five straight-edged cookie sheets can make a reflector oven (Figure 8-8). Three cookie sheets hinged together like a binder make the top and bottom of the oven and the center shelf. Bolt the sides of the top and bottom (which are at a right angle to

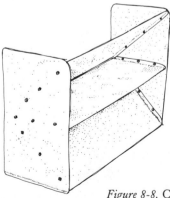

Figure 8-8. Cookie sheet reflector oven

each other and at a 45° angle to the ground) to the sides of the oven, which are the fourth and fifth cookie sheets. Bolt the sides of the horizontal center shelf to the sides of the oven. The cookie sheet reflector oven is complete.

Sheet Metal Reflector Oven

Cut three rectangles of sheet metal of equal size and attach them together along one long side with metal rings, like a binder (Figure 8-9). Open out the three metal sheets so the top and bottom sheets are at right angles to each other and the center sheet is horizontal. Holding each sheet in this position, lash each (with wire inserted through holes drilled in the corners of the sheets) to metal stakes or green sticks set in the ground on either side of the reflector oven. Cover the open sides of the oven with foil for additional reflected heat.

Figure 8-9. Sheet metal reflector oven

Care

Keep the reflector oven clean and shiny to create the most effective heat reflection. If the metal won't clean well, cover the oven with the shiny side of the aluminum foil outward so that it will reflect better.

Foods

Any foods that can be baked in 30 minutes or less in an oven can be baked in the out-of-doors in a reflector oven. Cookies, brownies, biscuits, pizza and cake are some of the favorites.

Steps

Place the food on a piece of foil or a pan that will fit on the shelf of the reflector oven, then place the oven near the fire. Knowing just where to place the reflector oven so it will heat to the right temperature is the real key to cooking effectively. An oven thermometer inside the oven works well. Do not place it on top of the oven because it will catch the rising hot air and register a higher temperature than the shelf temperature. It is possible to learn to guess the temperature with reasonable accuracy by holding your hand just in front of the oven. If you can hold it there for only 1 or 2 seconds, the temperature is near 500° F. If you can hold it there for 3 to 4 seconds, 400° F; 6 seconds, 300° F; and 7 to 10 seconds, 200° F.

After the food has been cooking for 5 minutes, check it to make sure that it is cooking properly. Just lift the oven away from the fire area. Sometimes the food cooks faster at the front of the oven than it does at the back. If this happens, check to make sure that the oven is not too hot. Turn the food occasionally so it will cook more evenly. If the top of the food is browning faster than the bottom, the fire is too large. Similarly, the fire is too small if foods are browner on the bottom than on the top.

Cardboard Box/Foil Oven

The efficiency of this oven will delight you. It will bake a cake as good as if it were baked at home. The oven is fun to make, too, before you start out on your camping trip (Figure 8-10).

- Cut the top off of a cardboard box approximately 1 foot square. (The box should be about 1 inch larger all the way around than the baking pan that will be used inside it.) With the top cut off, the box should be laid on its side. The cut-off portion of the box will be the opening to the oven.
- Line the entire inside of the box with foil.
- Close all seams on the outside of the box with duct tape (heat-resistant tape) to keep heat from leaking out.
- Punch two holes on both sides of the box near the bottom, about ¼ inch in diameter for ventilation. If the coals don't continue to burn, you may have to punch more holes.
- Punch two small holes quite close together at the back, high in one corner. Insert a twisty (from a plastic bag) through one

Figure 8-10. Cardboard box/foil oven

Figure 8-11. Cake in a cardboard box oven

hole. Put the other end through the hole inside the box and place a thermometer through the loop made by the twisty. Pull the twisty, and twist the ends together.

For the door of the oven, cut a piece of cardboard about ¼ inch larger than the hole to the oven. Line the inside of the door with foil. On the outside of the door, tape a handle shaped from cardboard.

- If you want a window in the oven door, cut a square hole in the door and cover it with transparent oven wrap secured by the duct tape.
- Secure the door to the top of the opening with duct tape so the door swings free, as if it were hinged.
- To make the rack inside the oven, use a rack about 20 inches long and 6 inches wide. Your local hardware store should have this type of rack material. Fold both ends of the rack, about 4½ inches in from the ends, at right angles—your flat surface will be 11 inches—and stand the rack inside the oven.
- For insulation, pour pebbles or dirt into a pan that will fit into the bottom of the oven. (Foil can be placed across the dirt or sand to elevate the briquets a little bit so more oxygen can get to the briquets.) Place fifteen to twenty hot briquets on top of the pebbles.

When you are ready to use the oven, preheat it to the desired heat. When the food is placed on the rack (Figure 8-11), the temperature will go down temporarily but should rise as the food cooks. Place a rock against the outside of the oven door to keep it closed (Figure 8-12). A small gap is okay, but large spaces will let the heat out. The briquets will hold their heat for about 1 hour. If you expect to use the oven for a longer period of time, add briquets gradually while the first ones are still hot.

Cardboard Box Oven With a Window

Cut the top and bottom from a cardboard box about 12 inches square and 14 inches deep. Cover the bottom edge of the cardboard box with aluminum foil so it will be protected from the heat of the coals (Figure 8-13).

Dig a small trench 8 inches deep, 8 inches wide and about 18 to 20 inches long. Place charcoal briquets in one end of the trench and light them. (See pages 64-66 for more on how to start charcoal briquets.)

Place a cooling rack in the middle of the box. Poke a hole above and below each corner of the rack and wire the rack in place. The box is placed over the charcoal briquets in the open trench that extends from under the box and admits needed air to the coals. The edge of the box, even though it is reinforced with additional foil, should be kept away from direct heat as much as possible.

Figure 8-12. Cardboard box oven while baking

Figure 8-13. Cardboard box oven with a window

Figure 8-14. Bread baking in cardboard box oven with a window

Place the item to be baked or roasted on the upper cross wires and cover the box with a roasting wrap (secured with either string or a rubber band) so you can see the food baking (Figure 8-14). Aluminum foil can be used, but it won't allow you to watch the food cooking. The oven can be lifted on and off the coals as needed. If desired, a portable oven thermometer can be hung on the upper inside of the box to determine the heat of the oven.

Outdoor Appliances for Enclosed and Concentrated Heat Cooking

Figure 8-15. Enclosed heat circulating inside Dutch oven

Figure 8-16. Enclosed heat circulating inside tin can stove oven

Figure 8-17. Enclosed heat circulating inside can-inside-can oven

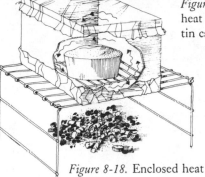

Figure 8-18. Enclosed heat circulating in cardboard box oven

Figure 8-19. Enclosed heat circulating in loaf in tin-can oven

Figure 8-20. Concentrated heat in reflector oven

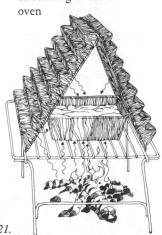

Figure 8-21. Concentrated heat foil-pan oven

Recipes for Enclosed and Concentrated Heat

Hot meals — breakfasts, lunches, dinners, from appetizers to desserts — you can cook them all in the wilderness. Here are some recipes for you to begin with, using the enclosed or concentrated (oven) method. Try your own favorites, too!

DUMP CAKE

Method: *Dutch oven (For easy cleaning, line Dutch oven with foil)*
Time: *45 minutes to 1 hour*

- Place in Dutch oven

  1 29-ounce can sliced peaches with juice

- Dump over top of peaches and spread evenly

  1 white or yellow cake mix

- Stir enough to moisten cake mix.
- Dot top with

  ¼ pound butter or margarine

Place coals on top and bottom of Dutch oven and bake for 45 minutes.

Variations: Pineapple, cherries, apples and other fruits may be substituted for the peaches. Nuts can also be sprinkled over the top. The flavor of the cake may also be varied. Serves 6 to 8.

GOURMET GERMAN PANCAKES

Method: *12-inch Dutch oven (with 3 ¾-inch rocks in bottom) and 1 pie pan*
Time: *15 minutes*

- In pie tin placed on rocks in bottom of Dutch oven, melt

  1 tablespoon butter

- Pour into pie tin ¼-inch deep batter made by mixing

  3 eggs
  ½ cup flour
  ½ cup milk
  dash of salt

Put lid on oven and place on bed of coals, with several coals on top of lid. (The Dutch oven must be very hot, equal to a 400° F oven.)

Cook for 10 to 15 minutes, then remove lid. The pancake batter will have risen up the sides and browned. Divide into the number of portions to be served and place a mixture of drained raspberries, sliced bananas and chunk pineapple (or other types of fruit) on the pancake, sprinkle with brown sugar and dot with sour cream. Serves 3.

DEEP-PAN PIZZA

Method: *Pie pan oven*
Time: *20 minutes*

• Fry in saucepan or Dutch oven	½ pound hamburger
• Oil	1 pie pan
• Cover other pie pan and its sides with	1 or 2 flour tortillas
• Add cooked meat.	
• Pour to ⅓-inch deep into tortillas	1-2 cups spaghetti sauce
• Dice and add to the spaghetti sauce and meat	½ green pepper and ½ onion
• Slice or grate and cover all of the above with	½ pound mozzarella cheese

Turn the empty pie pan lid upside down and clamp to bottom pie pan. Place on rocks above coals and put hot coals on top. Cook until green pepper and onions are softened. Cut pizza with a knife and remove with a spatula. Serves 2.
Variation: Substitute any of your favorite pizza ingredients for any of the above.

DUTCH OVEN ROAST BEEF

Method: *Dutch oven*
Time: *3 to 4 hours*

• Braise	1 pot roast
• Add	1 can consomme (10½ ounces)
• Add	5 carrots
	3-4 potatoes
	1 onion
	salt and pepper
	½ package dried onion soup

Place lid on Dutch oven, leaving a space between the meat and the lid. Place the Dutch oven in the fire pit that has been lined with dry rocks and has had a glowing fire for about 1 to 1½ hours. Cover with coals. Depending on size of roast, it should be cooked in 2½ to 3½ hours. Gravy can be made from juices by adding flour to cold water to make a smooth paste. Pour through a small strainer to thicken gravy. Serves 6.

PISTOL ROCK CHICKEN

Method: *Dutch oven*
Time: *2 hours*

- Rinse and pat dry with paper towel   1 whole chicken, cut up and skinned

- In a single layer, place chicken inside a jumbo self-sealing bag.
- Add

  salt
  pepper
  garlic salt
  1 cup flour

- Close bag and shake well to coat chicken with flour.
- Pour in warm Dutch oven   2 tablespoons oil
- Brown the chicken.
- Pour over top of chicken

  3 14½-ounce cans pasta sauce
  1 8-ounce can sliced mushrooms, drained

Let simmer for 1 to 1½ hours until the sauce thickens and the chicken is tender. Serves 4.

SLOPPY JOE BISCUIT BAKE

Method: *Dutch oven*
Time: *30-40 minutes*

- In Dutch oven, brown

  1 large onion
  2 pounds lean ground beef

- Once meat has browned, add

  2 packages (1.3 ounces each) Sloppy Joe seasoning mix
  2 6-ounce cans tomato paste
  2 cups water

- Stir well and bring to a boil.
- Place over meat mixture

  1 16-ounce package refrigerator biscuits

Bake for 15 to 20 minutes until the biscuits are browned. Serves 4 to 6.

COWBOY POTATOES

Method: *Dutch oven*
Time: *1 to 1½ hours*

• Brown in Dutch oven	12 slices bacon, diced
• After bacon has browned, remove and drain on paper towel.	
• Brown	3 medium onions, diced
• Add	12 medium potatoes, sliced
	salt
	pepper
• Cover and cook 35 to 45 minutes until potatoes are tender.	
• Add and stir in	1 to 2 cups frozen peas
	bacon bits (to taste)
• Sprinkle over top	2 cups cheddar cheese, grated

Cover and let the cheese melt. Serves 8 to 10.

PINEAPPLE UPSIDE-DOWN CAKE

Method: *Dutch oven*
Time: *1 hour*

• After lining Dutch oven with foil, melt in the bottom	3 tablespoons butter or margarine
• Arrange on the bottom	1 20-ounce can sliced pineapple
• In center of each pineapple, place a	maraschino cherry
• Sprinkle over top of pineapple and cherries	½ cup brown sugar
• Combine and mix	1 package yellow cake mix
	1¼ cups water
	⅓ cup oil
	3 eggs

Pour cake mix over the fruit mixture and bake for 35 to 40 minutes. Serves 8.

RICE PUDDING

Method: *Dutch oven*
Time: *30 minutes*

- Mix together

2 cups cooked rice
4 cups milk
½ cup brown sugar
½ teaspoon cinnamon
½ cup raisins
2 eggs, beaten
pinch of salt
1 teaspoon vanilla

Pour into greased Dutch oven. Leave about 1 inch of air space under the Dutch oven lid so milk does not scorch. Cover with lid. Place coals on top and around bottom of Dutch oven and bake. Serves 6 to 8.

BAKED EGGS

Method: *Muffin pan*
Time: *About 10 to 15 minutes*

- Into paper lined muffin pan, break

12 eggs

- Add to each egg

1 tablespoon milk
grated cheese
salt and pepper
½ slice cooked bacon, diced

Put another muffin pan over and clamp. Place over low-heat coals, and place coals on lid to bake. Use cupcake liners for cleaning ease. Serves 6.

CHEESY SNACKEROOS

Method: *Dutch oven*
Time: *Approximately 25 minutes*

- Prepare according to package instructions

1 package corn bread or corn muffin mix (8½ ounces)

- Add to this mixture

⅓ cup grated Parmesan cheese

- Place in well-greased Dutch oven.

- Sprinkle over the top
  - ¾ cup chopped salted peanuts
  - ⅓ cup grated Parmesan cheese
  - ½ teaspoon garlic salt
- Dot the top with
  - 2 tablespoons margarine

Cover Dutch oven. Bake over coals 25 minutes or until light brown. Cool slightly before cutting in wedges and serving. Serves 4.

Can Ovens

Can ovens are an enjoyable method of cooking. They are very good for the backpacker who wishes to "travel light," but they are usually small and should be used with groups of only two or three people.

Principle
Can ovens are used for baking foods. They are easily created by placing food inside one can or pan, then placing a larger can or other covering over the top to act as the oven. The trapped heat will circulate around the smaller can to cook the food.

Fire(s)
Coals are needed for can ovens. A log-cabin or crisscross fire will produce coals quickly, but charcoal briquets are also very effective.

Equipment and Preparation
The type of can oven you are making determines the equipment and preparation needed. Several types are suggested below.

Can Oven
A small can that fits inside another can may be used for baking. Special precautions should be taken not to place too many coals either below or on top of the can oven. Elevating the inside can on small rocks regulates the temperature better.

Arch Oven
A foil or can arch may be used to bake breads, pies, cakes or any food to be baked in the oven of a range. The arch is dome-shaped

to create a surface from which the heat will reflect. The arch may be made a couple ways.

1. *Foil arch*. Place a wire rack over the hot coals and put the food on it. Make an arch dome from heavy-duty foil. Place it over the grill with the shiny side toward the food. Fasten the foil down with a green stick, or wire it to the grill before placing the grill on the heat.
2. *Broiler-pan arch*. Broiler pans wired or taped together in a tepee shape also work well as an arch (Figure 8-22).

Figure 8-22.
Broiler pan arch

Can Over Can

Set a can of cake batter or other food on three stones in the hot coals (Figure 8-23). Place a larger tin can over the small can. Place coals around the larger can and let the food cook as long as it usually takes to cook in an oven.

Meat can be baked using this same principle. Skewer or wire the meat to a heavy stick, then hammer it vertically into the ground until it stands up alone. Cut the top out of a 5-gallon honey can, turn the can upside down over the meat on the stick, and push the can into the ground to seal the oven. Place coals around the can and on top of it and cook the meat about 1½ to 2½ hours. Remove the can and check the meat to see if it is done.

coals or charcoal briquets

briquets

rocks

Figure 8-23. Can over can oven

Figure 8-24. Can in a can oven

flat rock

Figure 8-25. Round can oven

Enclosed and Concentrated Heat—Your Camping Oven   137

Hang a Can in a Can

Use a #10 can, a 1-gallon can, a small coffee can (or another can of that size) and a wire hanger (Figure 8-24). Cut both ends out of the gallon can. Punch three holes in the top of the small can with a punch-type opener. Push the sharp edges into the can, out of the way. Cut three wires 4 to 6 inches long. Make a hook on one end of each wire that will hook over the top edge of the 1-gallon can and a hook on the other end that will hook the smaller can. Place the food in the small can and hook it into place inside the large can. Place the large can over the coals so that the small can rests about 3 inches above the coals. Cover the top of the large can with foil so heat will circulate around the small can, creating an oven. Coals can be placed on the foil if more heat is needed.

With a slight variation, this type of hanging can may also be used for frying. Punch holes in the small suspended can, place briquets in it, and place a frying pan on top of the large can.

Round Can Oven

Place the food to be cooked inside a loaf pan. Suspend a larger round can over hot coals and slide the loaf pan into the larger round can. Cover its opening with aluminum foil to create the oven and let the food bake (Figure 8-25).

CHAPTER 9

Stick and Spit Cooking: Cooking With Circulating Heat

Probably the most commonly used method of outdoor food preparation is stick cooking, which can be an exciting way to involve each camper in the preparation of his or her own meal. This method is most often used to prepare meats and breads. The combination of meat, fruits and vegetables prepared on a stick is commonly called the shish kebab.

Spit cooking is very similar to stick cooking. The main difference is in the amount of food to be cooked. Larger amounts of food can be cooked on a spit.

Stick and Spit Cooking

Principle
Much like using a broiler or a rotisserie at home where dry heat is used, food is placed on a stick, held near the coals and rotated until cooked.

Fire(s)
Always use hot coals to cook foods on a stick rather than direct flames. Good coals can be made from a crisscross fire or a log cabin fire (see chapter five on fire building). Charcoal briquets can also be used if coals are needed for a longer period of time.

For a spit, a large fire is good because you can have the needed amount of coals available all the time.

Equipment Needs: Stick Cooking

Either a stick, wood dowel or wire coat hanger is needed for stick cooking. Cut a straight green stick about ½ inch in diameter and 4 feet long; sharpen it to a point on one end. Willows, usually growing near stream beds, work well.

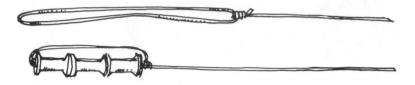

Figure 9-1. Coat hanger for stick cooking

Adapt a coat hanger for stick cooking by untwisting the hanger at the top and unfolding it until it is straight (Figure 9-1). To make a handle, place three empty thread spools on one end. Bend the wire, extending around them to the front of the spools, then turn the end around the wire to secure them onto the hanger. A shorter-handled stick can be made by straightening the hook for a place to put the food and pulling out the center of the bottom of the hanger to straighten it into a double-wire handle. This will make a stronger handle.

Equipment Needs: Spit Cooking

One method of spit cooking uses a stick about ¾-inch in diameter and 1 to 2 feet longer than the fireplace area. A small stick can be lashed onto this stick to make it easier to turn. It is a good idea not to strip the bark from the stick because food will slip more easily on a slick surface. Just wash the bark with soap and rinse it. Cut two forked sticks tall enough to hold the spit about 2 feet above the hot coals and pound into the ground on either side of the fireplace area (Figure 9-2). If there are flat rocks in the area, pile two stacks to take the place of the two forked sticks. Bricks can also be stacked. To keep the stick from rolling off the bricks, place one stick in each of the two brick holes on both sides. The spit will fit between the sticks to hold it securely.

Another method of spit cooking uses a pipe (Figure 9-3). If you are using a metal pipe, determine the length of it by the amount of food you plan to cook on the spit. Drill two or three holes in the center of the pipe for threading wire or heavy string

Figure 9-2. Spit cooking

Figure 9-3. Pipes used to make a spit

through to anchor the food to the pipe. A metal spit may have a handle welded on one end to make it easier to turn.

Use sturdy, green, forked sticks to hold the pipe, or prepare two pipes by welding three U-shaped pieces of half pipe to the sides of two 3-foot pieces of pipe. The three pipes will serve as brackets, making it possible to change the height of the spit. Stacked rocks or bricks also work well.

Care

Wooden sticks need to be burned or stacked neatly for other campers before you leave the campsite. Coat hangers may be cleaned easily either by placing the end of the wire in the hot coals to burn off the food or by using steel wool. If cleaned well after each use, this type of stick may be used over and over again. The metal spit equipment should be burned clean and wiped off for future use. Anything that is not kept should be properly disposed of.

Steps: Stick Cooking

Place the food(s) to be cooked on the stick or wire hanger. Hangers are good to use with shish kebabs because the food will slide easily onto the hangers. However, cut the food in small pieces so the hangers are not too heavy. Meats should be cut into thin strips and double threaded onto the wire. Heavy foods will not rotate on the hanger.

Place shish kebabs over the coals but not too near, or the food will be cooked on the outside and raw in the middle. If the food will take a long time to cook, find a rock to place under the stick near the handle and another to hold the stick down. Turn the stick periodically until the food is done.

If one item will take more time to cook than the others, it can be partially precooked. A good example of this would be the meat used for shish kebabs. The meat can be boiled or fried first.

Steps: Spit Cooking

Prepare the food to be placed on the spit by washing it, centering it on the pole and basting it with sauce. If the food needs to be wired to the pipe (or the pole), begin at one end and wire one item at a time, making sure to put the wire or string through the holes if you are using a pipe. Be sure to wire the legs and wings

DINGLE FAN ROASTER

The dingle fan roaster is an old pioneer method of roasting meat. It operates on the principle that the fan will move away from the hot air and twist the string as it moves. As the string twists and unwinds, it turns the roast so that the meat is browned on all sides. It is also twisted by the action of the wind or a slight breeze.

Rest a long pole on a large rock with one end of the pole, anchored to the ground by another heavy rock. The free end of the pole will rise into the air near the fire. To this end of the pole, attach a length of chain about 6 inches long, then tie a heavy piece of string to the end of the chain. Tie a loop for a hook at the end of the string.

Using wire or a green switch, make a loop about 9 inches in diameter and cover it with a bandanna (by placing the bandanna over the loop and tying the four ends of the bandanna with string and drawing them together) to form the dingle fan. Tie the handle of the loop (2 to 3 inches away from the fan) to the string just below the chain, and attach a chunk of wood or stone to the end of the handle (opposite the bandanna-fan) to counterbalance the fan.

Tie the roast or chicken with wire or heavy string, placing one hook at the top and another at the bottom of the meat, so it can be rotated. Place a foil pan under the meat to catch the drippings. Baste the meat occasionally until it is well done. Be sure to keep the fire burning; the hot air will keep the fan turning (Figure 9-4).

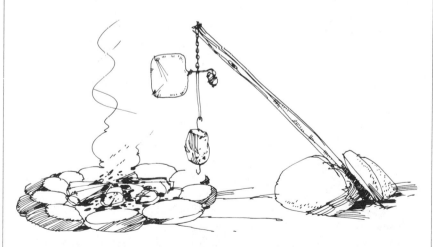

Figure 9-4. Dingle fan roaster

of a chicken tightly to its body so they will not burn.

Place the food over the coals and wait about 5 minutes to see if it is cooking properly. If it is cooking too fast, raise the spit; if too slow, lower it. Keep the food slowly rotating. Food that takes a long period of time to cook, such as chicken, can be rotated at intervals of 3 to 5 minutes.

Fun Types of Stick and Spit Cooking

Vertical Spit

Chicken and other items may be cooked with this method, which is like an uncovered oven.

- Drive four 3-foot-long metal stakes into the ground 12 to 14 inches apart, forming a square.
- Cut four pieces of 1-inch mesh chicken wire 2 feet long and nine holes wide (leave nine holes and cut the tenth in half).
- Fasten the two long sides of each roll together, making long, tube-like wire cages.
- Slip each wire cage vertically down over each metal stake and fill each wire cage with briquets—one row of briquets from the ground to the top of the cage (Figure 9-5).
- Light the briquets. After they are hot, wrap aluminum foil around the outside of the four stakes to hold the heat in the enclosed area (Figure 9-6).
- Make a tripod out of three sticks or lengths of metal about 4 feet long, tying them together at the top with rope.
- Place the tripod over the four stakes so that the top of the tripod is centered over them.
- Tie the wings and legs of a chicken (fryer) to its body.
- Tie a length of heavy string to the legs of the chicken long enough so that when the other end of the string is tied to the top of the tripod, the chicken will dangle about 3 to 4 inches above the ground (Figure 9-7).

It will take about 1 to 1½ hours to roast the chicken. When you baste the chicken with barbecue sauce, do it the last 15 minutes, or the sauce will burn. A turkey can also be cooked using this method; however, the stakes will have to be moved farther apart depending on the size of the bird.

Figure 9-5. Briquets in wire cages

Figure 9-6. Wrapping foil around a vertical barbecue

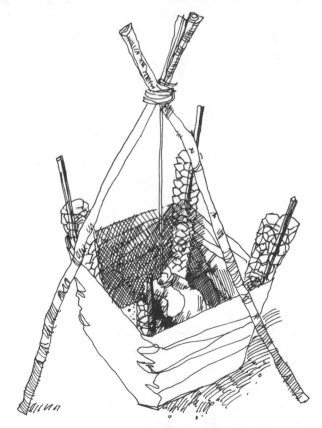

Figure 9-7. Tripod centered over stakes suspending a chicken

Stick and Spit Cooking: Cooking With Circulating Heat   145

Plank or Split-Log

Fish, steak or any meat about ½- to 1-inch thick can be cooked this way. (Fish cooks rather quickly this way.) Thicker pieces of meat will have to be removed and turned to finish cooking.

- Use a clean board or split a piece of firewood at least 6 inches in diameter.
- Outline the meat on the board at intervals with nails. With string, lace from nail to nail across the meat to hold it in place.
- Baste with oil and salt.
- Place the meat toward the fire, not too near, or the wood might catch fire.

Fish-on-a-Stick

Tired of fish-in-a-frying-pan? Try a more natural way, with no dishes to wash afterward.

- Clean your fish, leaving its head on.
- Sharpen both ends of a sweet-bark stick about the circumference of your finger and 6 inches longer than the fish.
- Thrust one end of the stick through the fish's mouth, up inside near the backbone, and into the flesh of the tail.
- Rub the fish with oil.
- Wrap foil around the exposed end of the stick to prevent it from burning.
- Push the free end of the stick into the ground near the fire until the fish's head nearly touches the ground.
- Push the coals toward the stick, being careful not to let them touch the stick, or it will burn.
- Cook for about ½ hour, or until the fish is done. The head of the fish may scorch or burn a little, but you won't want to eat that part anyway.

Recipes for Stick Cooking

Stick cooking is perhaps the most popular method of cooking in the out-of-doors because it is easy and quick, with very little cleanup afterward. Another reason for its popularity is that it is one method of cooking unique to the out-of-doors. Try the following recipes on your family.

Figure 9-8. Cooking an egg on a stick

EGG ON A STICK

Method: *Stick cooking*

Time: *20 to 30 minutes*

- With a pin or the point of a sharp knife, carefully tap a small hole in one end of   1 egg
- Sharpen to an even thickness no larger than ³⁄₁₆ inch   1 small stick

Insert sharpened stick into the hole in the egg and through to the other end. Now carefully tap another small hole to let the stick come through. Balance the stick on a rock near the fire so the egg is approximately 6 inches above the coals. Turn in 10 to 15 minutes to cook the other side. Serves 1 (Figure 9-8).

Figure 9-9. Making slits in a marshallow for inserting chocloate chips

Figure 9-10. Fitting the marshmallows and chocolate chips together on a stick

Figure 9-11. Marshmallows and melted chocolate chips between graham crackers

NEW METHOD FOR S'MORES

Method: *Stick cooking*

Time: *3 minutes*

- With a sharp knife, cut slits in the four corners of the flat side of .... 1 marshmallow
- In the slits, insert (sharp end first) .... 4 milk chocolate chips
- Repeat with .... 1 marshmallow
- Fit the chocolate chip ends of the two marshmallows together, slide them onto the sharp end of a stick and toast them slowly over .... hot coals
- When the marshmallows are golden brown, sandwich them between .... 2 graham crackers

This method guarantees melted chocolate, so you'll really want s'more. Serves 1. (See Figures 9-9, 9-10 and 9-11.)

MEAT LOAF ON A STICK (DRUMSTICKS)

Method: *Stick cooking*

Time: *20 to 30 minutes*

- Crush .... 1 cup cornflakes
- Mix together with .... 1 pound hamburger
  - 1 egg
  - ½ onion (chopped)
  - 2 teaspoons salt
  - ⅛ teaspoon pepper
  - 1 teaspoon mustard

Wrap a small quantity of this mixture around the end of a stick, making it long instead of into a round ball. Wrap foil around the meat and part of the stick to prevent the meat from falling into the coals. Place it over a bed of coals, turning it slowly to cook it evenly. Makes about seven drumsticks. Serves 3 to 4. (See Figures 9-12 and 9-13 on page 150.)

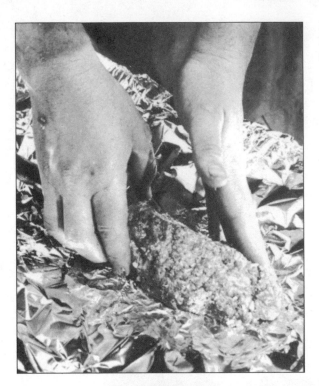

Figure 9-12.
Preparing the
meat loaf

Figure 9-13.
Cooking the
meat loaf on a
stick

Roughing It Easy

APPLE PIE ON A STICK

This is a wonderful treat to have while you are enjoying a camp-fire. You will need an apple and roasting stick or dowel for each person, and a bowl with 1 cup of sugar and 1 tablespoon of cinnamon mixed in it. The best apples to use are cooking apples such as Jonathan or Rome because when they are warm, the skins are easy to peel off.

To begin, push the stick or dowel through the top of the apple until the apple is secure on the stick. Place the apple 2 to 3 inches above the hot coals and turn the apple while roasting it. As the apple cooks, the skin starts to brown and the juice comes out. When the skin is loose, remove the apple from the fire but leave it on the stick. Peel the skin off the apple, being careful not to burn yourself since the apple is very hot (Figure 9-14). Roll the apple in the sugar and cinnamon mixture, then return it to roast over the coals, letting the sugar and cinnamon heat to form a glaze over the apple (Figure 9-15). Remove the apple from the coals and let it cool. Then slice off pieces and eat your "apple pie on a stick."

Figure 9-14. Peeling the scorched skin off the apple

Figure 9-15. Rolling the apple in cinnamon and sugar

CHAPTER 10

Dutch Oven Cooking

Dutch oven cooking is one of the oldest and most popular types of cooking in the out-of-doors. A Dutch oven is probably the most versatile piece of cooking equipment available. The Dutch oven is a heavy, flat-bottomed, cast-iron or aluminum kettle with a close-fitting lid and a sturdy handle. Varying in size from 8 to 16 inches in diameter and 4 to 6 inches in depth, it has heavy sides (about ⅓ inch thick) that hold heat evenly for a long period of time.

Principle

The Dutch oven is a piece of equipment that can be used in a variety of cooking methods. It is ideal for shallow frying, deep fat frying, roasting, baking and stewing. Therefore, you may cook with either dry heat or moist heat.

There are two types of ovens, the outdoor and the indoor (Figures 10-1 and 10-2). The outdoor oven has three legs, designed to hold the oven above hot coals and to allow air circulation below it. It has a relatively flat lid with a handle and turned-up edges so hot coals can be placed on it. The indoor oven is without legs so it may rest on a flat stove. Its lid is round and

Figures 10-1 and 10-2. Outdoor and indoor Dutch ovens

Roughing It Easy

without raised edges. This oven can be converted for outdoor cooking by supporting it above the coals with three rocks or bricks. To help the lid hold coals, make a foil ring a little smaller in circumference than the lid. Set the foil on the lid and place hot coals inside the ring. The lid can also be turned upside down to hold hot coals.

If a Dutch oven is not available, a large kettle from a camp cooking set can also be used; however, it will not hold heat as well and foods tend to burn more easily.

Fire(s)

The Dutch oven is designed to be hung over open-flame fires, placed on the ground over coals, or buried underground in coals.

Open Flame

A tepee fire or a lazy man's fire can be used when the Dutch oven is used as a kettle. The kettle is hooked to a tripod and hung over the open fire like a spit. It can also be hooked onto the end of a pole that is placed on a large rock, with another heavy rock anchoring it down at the other end.

Coals

A keyhole fire is excellent for Dutch-oven cooking because you can move the coals in and out of the cooking area as needed (see chapter five). A good formula for determining the number of briquets to add to the Dutch oven is based on the size of the Dutch oven: add three more briquets to the top than the size of the oven, and three fewer to the bottom. This will give you an approximately 325° F oven.

Charcoal Briquets

If you are using charcoal briquets to make coals, place the number of briquets on both the top and bottom of the Dutch oven according to the following suggestions. Leave about a 2-inch-square space between briquets, forming a checkerboard pattern.

Size of Oven	Top	Bottom
8 inch	11	5
10 inch	13	7
12 inch	15	9
14 inch	17	11
16 inch	19	13

Because charcoal briquets give off a great deal of heat, check the food periodically until you're sure how many briquets on both the top and bottom will give the right amount of heat for the recipe you are cooking. When you are using more than one Dutch oven, stack them in order to save briquets. Bake items in the lower ovens, and fry foods in the top one (Figure 10-3).

Figure 10-3.
Stacked Dutch ovens

Underground
The Dutch oven works well in pit cooking for variety meals, one-pot meals or stewing. See pages 109-112 on pit cooking for further details.

Care of Equipment
Although it is very sturdy, the cast-iron Dutch oven can be broken if it is dropped or hit with something very heavy. Cold water on the hot oven might also break it or warp it. Thus, proper preparation and care of a Dutch oven is important.

Seasoning
Seasoning a cast-iron Dutch oven when it is new will help prevent rusting. Place the oven in the campfire or in your oven at home and warm it. Remove it from the heat and rub every area inside and outside with cooking oil or shortening. Place the Dutch oven back in the fire or in your oven at 350° F for 1 to 2 hours. Turn the oven off and do not open the door. Allow it to cool slowly. An old, rusty Dutch oven can be renovated by cleaning it well and seasoning it as just described.

Cleaning

Cast iron can be cleaned with a very mild soap or placed on the fire, letting the food burn off and wiping it with an oiled paper towel. If your oven at home has a self-cleaning temperature, use that for cleaning a *cast-iron* Dutch oven, and after cleaning, be sure to re-season the pan. It is good to oil the Dutch oven after each use. Take care not to overheat an aluminum Dutch oven; it may melt. Aluminum Dutch ovens can be cleaned with soap and water and seasoning is not necessary.

Foods

The Dutch oven can be used for cooking many different kinds of foods by several different methods. Frying and deep frying methods use heat only on the bottom. Baking, roasting and stewing require an oven-type heat created by placing coals both on the lid and below the Dutch oven.

Steps

Deep-Fat Frying

To deep-fat fry, place oil in the Dutch oven and set the oven over hot coals. If the oil heats up too much, remove it from the heat and wait until it cools. Fish and chips, chicken, fritters and corn dogs are a few foods that cook well this way.

Frying

The Dutch oven is excellent for frying food because it holds heat well. Begin frying when a drop of flour sizzles when placed in the oil.

The lid to the outdoor Dutch oven can be converted to a shallow frying pan by hammering three or four spikes into the ground, placing coals under the lid, and putting the lid topside down on the spikes (Figure 10-4). Rocks or bricks may be used in place of spikes. The Dutch oven may also be placed upside down with coals or briquets placed on its bottom, while the lid, also turned upside down, rests on the legs of the Dutch oven.

Boiling

Adjust the kettle above the coals. Move the coals around so the water is at a slow boil rather than at a rolling boil. The temperature of the water is the same at both stages of boiling, but when food is cooked at a vigorous boil, it breaks up more readily.

Figure 10-4.
Tall spikes

Stewing

Before stewing meat, brown it. Then add the liquids and the vegetables. With hot coals above and below the oven, this meal will cook without much help from the camp cook.

Roasting

Before roasting meat, warm the oven. Then add vegetable oil. Next, sear the meat on all sides and slowly pour about ½ to 1 cup of warm or hot water over it. Cold water will warp the oven. The water will allow the meat to self-baste in the cooking process. Season the meat as desired. Cover the oven with the lid and surround it with coals.

This is a good method for cooking large pieces of meat. Vegetables may be added when the meat is partially done. It is best to cook at a moderate heat.

Baking

For easy cleaning, place a layer of foil inside the Dutch oven and then place the food in the foil to bake it. This is a good way to bake cakes, upside-down cakes, biscuits, pies and apples (Figure 10-5). Allow approximately the same amount of cooking time in the Dutch oven as you would in your oven at home.

If you have two foods in smaller amounts to prepare at the same time, place rocks in the center as dividers and make two foil pans inside the Dutch oven. (See Figures 10-6, 10-7, and 10-8 on page 158.)

You may also use two pans in the Dutch oven. Cook together, for example, a meat loaf and scalloped potatoes or carrots (Figure

Figure 10-5. Cake in a foil-lined Dutch oven

10-9). Foods cooked in this manner should, of course, require about the same amount of cooking time; otherwise, they should be placed in the Dutch oven at different times.

Food can also be placed in a separate pan and set in the Dutch oven to cook. (Pies and cakes can be baked very successfully in this way.) Place four or five small flat rocks or three jar rings in the bottom of the Dutch oven to set the pan on. The rocks or rings will elevate the pan so heat may circulate around the food to cook it evenly and to keep it from burning. See pages 129-135 for Dutch oven recipes. For additional Dutch oven information, see the catalog section at the end of this book.

Figure 10-6. Shrinking Dutch oven area

Figure 10-7. Dividing Dutch oven area

Figure 10-8. Area divided with rocks and foil

Figure 10-9. Two pans in a Dutch oven

CHAPTER 11

Solar Heat

Solar heat box cooking is becoming more popular every day. Try your hand at making a solar reflector stove and/ or a solar oven. You'll be excited with the results.

Solar Reflector

A stove made of paper sounds about as practical as a pitcher carved from ice, but a paper stove is our project. Constructed almost entirely from cardboard, this reflector cooker will broil steaks, grill hot dogs, fry bacon and eggs, and make hotcakes and coffee. It will also heat the water for doing the dishes. All that's necessary is clear weather, because this stove cooks with sunshine! (Figure 11-1)

Figure 11-1. Solar reflector cooker

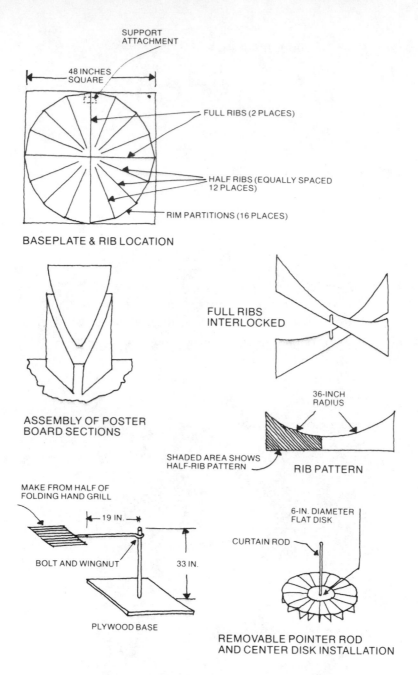

SUPPORT
ATTACHMENT

48 INCHES
SQUARE

FULL RIBS (2 PLACES)

HALF RIBS (EQUALLY SPACED
12 PLACES)

RIM PARTITIONS (16 PLACES)

BASEPLATE & RIB LOCATION

ASSEMBLY OF POSTER
BOARD SECTIONS

FULL RIBS
INTERLOCKED

36-INCH
RADIUS

SHADED AREA SHOWS
HALF-RIB PATTERN

RIB PATTERN

MAKE FROM HALF OF
FOLDING HAND GRILL

19 IN.

BOLT AND WINGNUT

33 IN.

PLYWOOD BASE

6-IN. DIAMETER
FLAT DISK

CURTAIN ROD

REMOVABLE POINTER ROD
AND CENTER DISK INSTALLATION

Figure 11-2. Plans for a solar reflector cooker

Stop to think about it for a minute, and you'll remember that every time we cook—whether it is with gas, electricity or charcoal—we indirectly use the sun's energy, which has been stored up and reconverted to heat. Sun-dried foods have long been eaten, and crude solar stoves were built a century ago. Besides, who hasn't heard of cooking an egg on the sidewalk on a really hot day?

Materials (Figure 11-2)

- Cardboard—as required
- Posterboard—six sheets, 22×28 inches
- Aluminum foil—one roll, heavy-duty, 18×37 inches
- Plywood—one piece, 18×24 inches
- ¾-inch aluminum tubing—approximately 64 inches
- ¾-inch mounting flange—one
- Grill—one
- Curtain rod—one
- Broomstick—4 feet
- Clothesline—1 foot
- Glue—as required
- Masking tape—as required
- $^3/_{16} \times 1$-inch bolt with wing nut—one set
- Wrapping paper

The reflector framework is cut from cardboard, approximately $^3/_{16}$-inch thick, the kind large cartons are made from. Some posterboard and aluminum foil will complete the cooker itself. A grill (for hot dogs, hamburgers or pans) is made from plywood, some tubing and an inexpensive hand grill that costs about 50 cents. Study the plans first to get the overall picture and determine how much new material will be needed.

The other items will be easy to find. Get all the materials ready and begin construction. An eager beaver can do the job in a day or so and begin sampling outdoor cooking á la sun right away.

A word about the principle of our reflector cooker will be helpful before we proceed any further. The reflector cooker simply focuses all the sun's rays that strike its surface onto the bottom of the grill. This is known as the focal point. Even on a clear winter day, the 12 square feet of area in our cooker collects a lot of warmth that becomes concentrated heat when shrunk into the 1-foot area of the grill.

Giant solar furnaces use curved reflectors. They generate thousands of degrees of heat at their focal points, using the same principle as our simple stove. To generate so much heat, they must be constructed accurately in a parabolic shape. This specially shaped curve reflects all the rays onto one tiny spot and gives the furnace a concentration ratio of many thousands to one. Obviously, we don't want such high temperatures — they would melt our pans!

Our reflector will use a radius of 36 inches instead of a true parabolic curve. This results in a larger spot at the focal point. And instead of one bowl-shaped reflector, we will use a number of wedge-shaped sections. Thus our focal point will be roughly the size of the cooking pan, which is just what we want. This model can be scaled down, but the heat won't be as intense.

Instructions

- First, cut a base piece 4-feet square from ³⁄₁₆-inch cardboard.
- Mark the layout of the reflector ribs right on this base (Figure 11-3). With a pencil and a piece of string, draw a circle 48 inches in diameter. This is the size of the finished cooker. Next draw two lines through the center of the base, perpendicular to each other as shown on the plans. These mark the location of the main ribs, which are made next.
- Draw two main ribs from a piece of cardboard 12 × 48 inches. Cut these carefully, using a sharp linoleum knife, a pocket-knife or a modeler's razor knife. Be sure to plan ahead so you won't waste material as you lay out the ribs. Each of the main ribs has a notch at the center. Notice that one is on the top and one on the bottom so they will interlock.
- Using a full rib as a pattern, mark out twelve half-ribs. Before cutting these, cement the full ribs to the base plate on the lines previously drawn. Model airplane glue or a good household cement will work well. Use straight pins to hold the ribs down and in place. Remove the pins when the cement is dry. While the parts are drying, cut out the remaining ribs.
- Three half-ribs fit between the quarter-sections of the circle. Glue these in place, lining up the end of each one with the circle you drew on the base plate.
- While the half-ribs are drying, cut the rectangular filler pieces of cardboard. These rim partitions fit between the outer tips of the ribs to complete the framework. These pieces should

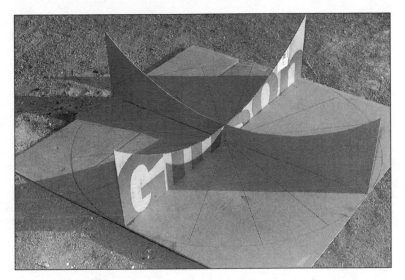

Figure 11-3. Base with glued-on cardboard ribs

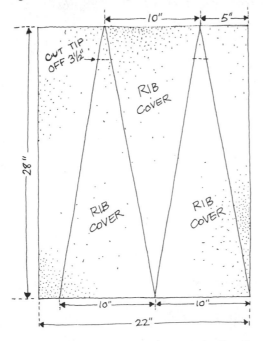

Figure 11-4. Marking rib covers on posterboard

be 12 inches high and approximately 9 to 9¼ inches wide. Each opening should be measured for proper fit. Fit each square together and tape the seams.

- When the framework is thoroughly dry, cut the wedge-shaped pieces of posterboard. (Since these form the curve that will reflect the sun's rays, use posterboard that's thin enough to bend easily, yet has sufficient body to hold the proper shape. Lighter cardboard tends to ripple and wave.) By marking a piece of posterboard as shown (Figure 11-4 on page 163), you will get three rib covers from each 22 × 28-inch sheet. Now cut 3½ inches off the tip to help the center fit better. Don't cement this in place yet; it will be the pattern for fifteen more pieces. Cut them carefully, making sure they will cover any of the spaces between the ribs. (In spite of your care, there may be slight inaccuracies in the framework.) It is better to have the posterboard pieces a bit too large than too small.

- Begin to cement the cut pieces into place. Since butting the joints smoothly against each other would be difficult, glue eight pieces in alternate spaces first (Figure 11-5). Spread glue along the tops of two ribs and the intervening filler piece, then lay the posterboard wedge in place and carefully press down so it touches the ribs at all points. The glue will dry enough in a minute or two that you can go on to the next piece. Don't forget to leave every other section open.

- Cover the open spaces with the remaining eight pieces of posterboard by running beads of cement along their edges. These eight pieces will, of course, lap over the edges of the pieces already glued in place, thus making a strong point. If you run into difficulty at the center where all the points come together, simply trim them off an inch or two. The hole left can be covered later with a separate piece of posterboard. Running masking tape along the seams will make a better glue joint and will hold the piece tight while it is drying (Figure 11-6).

- Cut a 6-inch circle out of posterboard and glue it over the center hole; tape the edges for reinforcement (Figure 11-7). Now you're ready to apply the aluminum foil that will give the reflector the mirrorlike finish necessary for collecting heat for cooking.

- Cut out 16 pieces of smooth-surfaced aluminum foil—the

Figure 11-5. Alternating wedges
glued onto ribs

Figure 11-6. Gluing and taping wedges

Figure 11-7. Gluing the circle over the center hole

Figure 11-8. Gluing foil to the wedges

Figure 11-9. Stick bracing the solar reflector

kind used in the kitchen for wrapping food. These should be slightly larger than the posterboard pieces to assure complete coverage of the reflector surface. Use rubber cement to stick the foil to the posterboard, and be sure to have the shiny side up (Figure 11-8). Work carefully and try to keep the foil smooth, but don't worry if the finished job isn't perfect. The cooker shown in the illustrations has a few ripples but works well anyway.

- Install a marker for the focal point of the reflector so you'll know where to place the grill for the fastest cooking. This is simply a small, inexpensive curtain rod of the type used on kitchen doors (Figure 11-9). It consists of two tubes, one fitted inside the other. Cut a short length of the larger tube and insert it into a hole punched in the center of the reflector. Better still, use a drill the same size as the tube or slightly smaller to give a snug fit. Now cement the tube in place. The smaller tube will fit into this "holder" and can be removed for easier handling when not needed.

- The focal point for our reflector is the proper place for mounting our grill. With a spherical reflector, the focal length is half the radius of the reflector, or in this case, 18 inches. As a double check, aim the reflector at the sun and adjust the tilt until there is no shadow visible from the pointer rod. Then hold a piece of wrapping paper with a small hole punched in it right at the tip of the pointer. Move the paper toward the reflector and then away from it until the smallest spot is observed on the paper. This is the actual focal point, and the pointer rod should be cut to this length.

- For support attachments, cut out two squares (2 × 2 inches) and one rectangle (2 × 6 inches) of cardboard, as shown by the dotted lines on the plans, and cement them to the center top back of the cardboard base. The squares go first, and then the rectangle. After these are well dried, run a short length of clothesline through the slot and tie the ends in a square knot. Drill holes through a 48-inch length of 1-inch dowel (broomstick or tubing), spacing the holes about an inch apart halfway down the dowel. Insert a nail to engage the loop of clothesline. You can now set up the reflector so it will stand alone.

- To make the grill, first cut a plywood base 18 × 24 inches. Any thickness from ½ to 1 inch will do. Mark the center and install a mounting flange for the ¾-inch vertical support, which is made of aluminum tubing 40 inches long, as shown in the plans.

- The adjustable arm is also aluminum tubing, 24 inches long. Flatten one end of the tubing as shown and bend it around a piece of pipe or a broomstick to make the collar, which fits over the vertical support. Drill a ³⁄₁₆-inch hole as shown, and insert a bolt and a wing nut. The other end of the adjustable arm can now be flattened. Keep the flat area at right angles to the collar so the grill will be horizontal when installed.
- Slide the grill into place, and the solar cooker is complete.
- Positioning the reflector is simple if you follow these directions. Stand behind it and face it right at the sun. Tilt it back until the shadow of the pointer rod vanishes as it did when we checked for focal length. This means that the reflector is aimed perfectly and that all the sun's rays will be bounced right where we want them.
- Holding the reflector in this position, slip the dowel or broomstick through the rope loop and put the nail through the hole just below the loop. With the reflector on its own feet you can now put the grill in place.
- Loosen the wing nut on the adjustable arm and move it up or down until the grill rests just above the tip of the pointer rod. As a double check, pass your hand quickly just above the grill. It should be hot, ready for you to start cooking.

How to Use Your Solar Cooker

The grill surface itself is fine for cooking hot dogs, hamburgers or steaks. Grease will drip onto the reflector but won't harm it. For bacon and eggs, hotcakes and the like, place a skillet on the griddle. If you like your steaks seared quickly to keep in the juice, use the skillet for them, too. By putting the skillet on the grill a few minutes early, you can store up extra heat that will cook the steak more rapidly.

Water can be heated in a kettle or pot. To get the maximum efficiency from your solar cooker, use blackened utensils, but just about any kind of utensil will work satisfactorily. For variety try using a pressure cooker.

Because the sun moves across the sky, the position of the

reflector will need to be adjusted as time passes. In the early morning or late afternoon, the reflector will be nearly vertical, while at noon you'll have to place it practically flat on the ground. That's why you drilled so many holes in the support rod. If you plan to boil beans or make stew, adjusting the reflector occasionally will keep the hot spot where it will do the most good. The shadow from the pointer rod is the thing to watch. For bacon and eggs, hot dogs and even steak, one setting will usually do the trick.

After cooking your meal and washing the dishes, remove the grill from the aluminum tube and clean it. Wipe off the reflector surface with a paper towel or damp cloth. That's all there is to the job of solar cooking.

Advantages of Solar Cooking

Of course, solar stoves won't take the place of other kinds of cooking all the time. When the sun goes down, you had better be through cooking, and on a rainy day, the reflector is not much use except maybe to crawl under to keep dry! But properly used in clear weather, a solar stove will amaze the most skeptical observer. Here are a few of the advantages of solar cooking:

- As you discovered when you held your hand close to the focal point, there is no warming-up period with a solar stove — it is hot right away! By the time the fellow with the charcoal brazier gets a good bed of coals, you will be doing the dishes.
- Besides, he paid for his fuel, while yours was free for the taking. Your solar method took nothing from the environment.
- And solar energy is available anywhere the sun shines — mountains, desert, beach or your own backyard.
- You'll notice how nice it is not to have your eyes full of smoke.
- Solar cooking is cool cooking, too, because the heat goes into the food on the grill and doesn't roast the person doing the cooking.
- You won't need matches to get your cooker going.
- There's no danger of setting anything on fire, either.
- There are no ashes or soot to contend with. If someone complains about the lack of charcoal or hickory taste, hand him a bottle of liquid smoke.

Seriously, you will have a lot of fun cooking with sunshine. It's safe, it's clean and it's free. Chances are you'll like it enough to want a portable cooker for your next camping trip, so you won't be tied down to a fireplace and the bother that goes with it. Save up for a commercial folding cooker, or put your ingenuity to work and make a portable version of the cardboard cooker.

The Solar Oven

The "greenhouse" effect is well known to those who have grown plants in such structures, and to any of us who have left the car windows rolled up on a warm, sunshiny day. The rays of the sun go through the glass well enough, but the reflections of a longer wavelength are unable to bounce back out of the car. The result is aptly described as resembling an oven. And that is just what you can build—a solar oven that will do a good job of cooking on a clear day, even in winter.

One aim of solar scientists is to provide a means of cooking for those countries in which fuel is scarce or expensive. Dr. Maria Telkes designed such an oven, which she feels might be mass-produced at a reasonable price. Our design is copied from the Telkes oven, which has been demonstrated in foreign lands.

Basically, the solar oven consists of a box for the food and a glass cover to admit and trap the heat inside the box (Figure 11-10). The box shown is made from galvanized iron but could well have been aluminum for lighter weight. The reflector panels are of aluminum.

You will need the sheet metal parts, a piece of double-strength window glass, a sealing strip for the glass, and three handles. The box is insulated with spun glass material 2 inches thick for greater heat retention.

Materials

- 28-gauge galvanized iron—16 square feet
- No. 6, ⅜-inch sheet metal screws—approximately twenty-four
- 2-inch Fiberglas insulation—12 square feet
- Double-strength window glass—22 × 24 inches
- Drawer pulls—three
- Flat black paint—one spray can

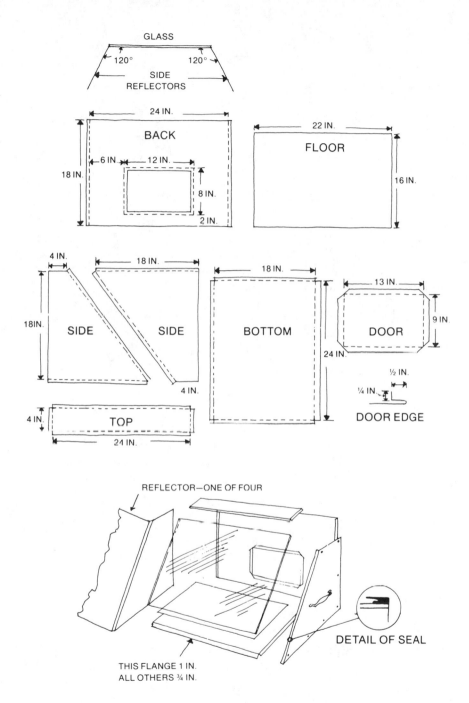

GLASS

120°   120°

SIDE
REFLECTORS

24 IN.

BACK

6 IN. — 12 IN.

18 IN.

8 IN.

2 IN.

22 IN.

FLOOR

16 IN.

4 IN.

18 IN.

18IN.   SIDE   SIDE

4 IN.

18 IN.

BOTTOM

24 IN.

13 IN.

DOOR   9 IN.

½ IN.

¼ IN.

DOOR EDGE

4 IN.   TOP

24 IN.

REFLECTOR—ONE OF FOUR

DETAIL OF SEAL

THIS FLANGE 1 IN.
ALL OTHERS ¾ IN.

Figure 11-10. Plans for the solar oven

- 2-inch roofing nails — six
- Sealer strip — 8 feet of ⅛ × 1-inch felt weather stripping or similar material
- Aluminum sheet .025 × 22 × 24 inches — four pieces

Again, it's a good idea to have all materials on hand before beginning the project. One exception might be the sheet metal for the box, in case you decide to let your local sheet metal shop do the cutting and bending for you. Unless you are familiar with metal work, having it done will produce a more professional job at little additional cost.

Instructions

If you want to do all the work yourself, and feel that you can handle the job, this is the way to begin.

Building the Exterior of the Oven

The bottom of the oven is a rectangle of metal, with the corners notched to allow you to bend up flanges all around the sides. These flanges are ¾ inch, and are bent up 90°, except for the front edge, which is a closed 45° angle, 1 inch long, as shown in the drawing.

The right and left side panels may be cut from one rectangle of metal to save material. Lay them out carefully to prevent waste. Again, flanges are bent ¾-inch wide at the front and top. The back and bottom edges are left flat. Be sure to make the bends opposite on each part so you'll have a right-hand panel and a left-hand panel, and not two of a kind!

The oven back has ¾-inch flanges on each side and an opening cut in it for the door. Notch the corners of the opening 45° and bend the ½-inch stiffener flanges in the same direction as the side flanges. This will strengthen the door opening and also give the back a finished appearance.

Now make the top of the box. This is a channel with one flange at 90° to fit the back and the other flange at 45° to match the slope of the glass. Next come two retaining angles 18 inches long, with ¾ × 1-inch legs. The box is now complete except for the door.

The door is the only difficult part to make. Care must be taken to bend it correctly. The double, or "hemmed" edge strengthens the door, and the flange left standing will fit into the opening in the back of the box. A snug fit will make for a neat, effective door that will seal properly and help keep the heat inside where we want it.

A false bottom is needed to prevent the insulation from collapsing under the weight of the food. This is a rectangle of metal sized as shown in the drawing. Make sure it's not so large that it contacts the front, sides or back of the box, causing heat loss by conduction to those parts.

It might be well to mention here that an alternate method of construction can be used, employing a little ingenuity and the do-it-yourself aluminum sheets and angles available at the hardware store. This method uses flat sheets, with angles attached to them instead of flanges bent from the sheets themselves. The 45° angles are eliminated, and a slightly different sealing technique is used for the glass, but some builders prefer doing it this way.

Assembling the Oven

Now, with the metal parts formed either in the sheet-metal shop or at your own workbench, you are ready to begin assembly of the oven.

The simplest way to put the oven together is with sheet metal screws. Use ⅜-inch screws for this purpose. They are available at the sheet metal shop or your hardware store. If you are using aluminum, substitute hardened aluminum screws, since different metals coming in contact with each other corrode.

Mark pencil guidelines ⅜-inch from the bottom edge of the side panels, spaced as shown on the drawing. Center-punch the holes and drill with a #40 drill. A hand drill is fine; an electric drill is even better for this purpose.

Now, with the bottom of the oven on a flat surface, hold the side panel against it and in its proper place. Drill through the holes in the side panel and into the flange of the bottom. It's a good idea to put a screw in each hole as it is drilled to ensure perfect alignment and prevent shifting of the parts. Notice that the bottom flange overlaps the side, but no holes are drilled at this point.

With both side panels attached to the bottom, the back of the box may now be put in place and holes drilled. Continue to insert screws as holes are drilled, carefully keeping the parts lined up as you progress.

Installing the Glass on the Front

The oven is taking shape now, and only the top needs to be added. Before you do this, however, you must install the glass on the front of the box. Take care not to break the glass. And don't cut your fingers on the edges.

Clean the glass carefully with water. Then glue the sealing strip around the edge with a good cement, following the directions to ensure a strong joint (Goodyear Pliobond® works well). If you find a sealer that fits over the edge of the glass, the job will be easy.

When the sealing strip is attached and properly set, put the glass in place in the oven. Slide it down through the top, which you have left open for this purpose. For this operation, lay the oven on its front face, making sure you have a perfectly flat surface to work on.

Next, install the 18-inch angles that hold the glass in place. Carefully drill holes in the sides of the box as shown in the drawing, locating them so they match the angles when put in position. Slip the angles through the opening in the top, and set them on the glass with the 1-inch leg flat against the side of the box.

Working from the top or reaching through the opening in the back of the box, press one angle very lightly against the glass. Don't force the glass so it flattens the sealing strip. This strip not only seals, but acts as a cushion to prevent breakage of the glass. Now, while holding the angle, mark through the holes in the side to indicate the proper location for the holes in the angle. Remove the angle, drill holes in it, then replace it and insert a sheet metal screw.

Repeat this process on the other side.

With the glass installed, the top can be put on and holes drilled through it and into the back and sides. Notice that the top fits over the back and side panels.

Adding the Final Details

The oven is now complete except for the carrying handles on each side and a similar handle on the door. These are attached with screws.

Fit the door into the opening, and mark the holes for the turn-buttons that hold the door tight. Drill $\frac{3}{16}$-inch holes in the back panel, and install the turn-buttons with nuts, bolts and washers. The washers hold the buttons away from the metal so they will clear the hemmed edge of the door.

Now cut spun-glass insulation to proper shape with a sharp knife or linoleum cutter. Use a straightedge for accurate trimming. Plan carefully so as not to waste material. The bottom piece can be leveled 45° at the front if care is taken.

Paint the inside surfaces of the insulation with flat black enamel. For convenience, use spray paint. After the paint is dry, the insulation is glued into the box with Pliobond or its equivalent. To do this, remove the back of the box and set it aside. Position the oven with the glass down, and cement the top insulation in place first and allow it to dry. Tip the box right side up, and cement the bottom insulation in place. Press five 2-inch roofing nails point-down into the insulation and lay the false bottom over them. This bottom piece is painted flat black, too.

The side insulation can now be cemented into place, and the box is complete except for the back. Cement insulation to the back panel, cut the small rectangle from the opening, and place it on the inside of the door. The back may now be carefully replaced and the screws inserted.

Put in an oven thermometer, fasten the door in place, and you are ready for the reflector panels, which are hinged to the box as shown in the drawing. (See Figure 11-10 on page 171.)

The Aluminum Reflector Plates

In tests, boxes built from this design have reached inner temperatures of only about 250° F. Heat loss to the surrounding air prevents the temperature inside from climbing higher. If we increase the amount of heat going into the box, the oven will get hotter. For this reason, we add the aluminum reflector plates. Use Alclad® if it is available.

Rivet two hinges to each reflector. Be sure to have two reflectors hinged on the ends and two hinged on the sides. If the Alclad sheets have red lettering on one side, use the opposite side for the reflecting surface. Attach the hinges to the box with sheet metal screws, installing the bottom reflector, then the sides, and

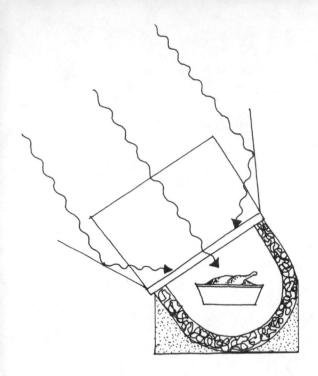

Figure 11-11. Solar oven angled to receive rays of sun

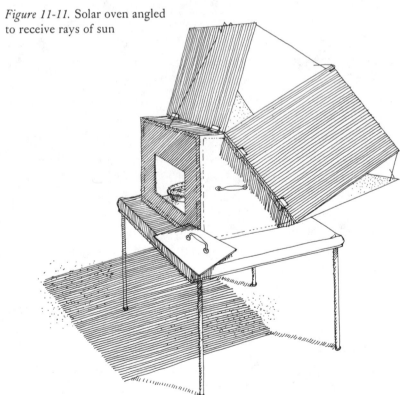

Figure 11-12. Pie baking in a solar oven

finally the top. Besides their primary purpose, the reflectors also protect the glass.

Open the side panels to an angle of 30° to receive the rays of the sun and reflect them into the box. Face the oven directly toward the sun, and this angle will always suffice for the side reflectors. A 45° tilt of the glass is a compromise angle that gives all-around performance. However, a little thought will tell us that for maximum performance, the angle of the top and bottom reflectors will vary with the position of the sun in the sky (Figure 11-11).

Adjusting the oven is simpler than it sounds. Set it out in the sun, preferably on a wooden table, and face it toward the sun. Open all the reflectors. Now swing the top reflector up and down while watching the inside of the oven. You will be able to tell when you have it at the proper angle by the reflection of the sun's rays on the dull black insulation.

Bend the end of a piece of galvanized wire to act as a stop, insert this wire in a hole in the top reflector, and wrap the free end around the loosened screw as shown in the illustration (Figure 11-12).

Swing the side reflectors into position, checking the angle they make with the glass by means of a cardboard template. Using two wires, attach the side reflectors to the top reflector. Now swing the bottom reflector up, watching the inside of the oven again. When it is properly positioned, fix two wires in place from the bottom reflector to the side reflectors, and the oven is ready.

The oven will reach a temperature of 350° F in 15 minutes. This was tested in Arizona in mid-January, when the air temperature was in the low 60s. The first time it was used, it baked a loaf of bread in just over an hour, and then cooked a 3-pound roast in 3½ hours! A whole meal can be cooked in the solar oven.

CHAPTER 12

Backpacking

Lightweight camping provides many advantages for anyone with an urge to backpack into the wilderness, hike across the dusty desert, ski cross-country in the cold of winter, bicycle off the beaten path, canoe on an exciting river or challenge the high mountains.

Perhaps the greatest joy of lightweight camping springs from that rediscovered sense of privacy and oneness with nature. You'll find yourself much more dependent on the elements and assuming more responsibility — both for yourself and the ecology of the land. There is a physical joy, too, in testing your own abilities and meeting your own goals. If you travel with others, close ties of companionship develop as you travel and work together. You'll also be able to see and live in country inaccessible to the automobile camper.

If you are a novice backpacker (and even if you are not), the question always is, "How little can I manage to take and still have everything I need?" This chapter should help you make some decisions about such items as backpacks, stoves, cooking equipment and miscellaneous items.

Types of Backpacks

There are three types of packs to choose from: day packs/fanny packs, internal frame packs and external frame packs. You must consider such factors as the amount and kinds of gear taken, the terrain and the duration of the trip.

Day Packs/Fanny Packs

Day packs can be used for anything from carrying books to school to extended ski excursions. Day packs range in size from 1,200 to 2,500 cubic inches and have a simple waist strap to keep them from swinging while you walk. Some feature an outside water bottle pocket and sternum strap. The material is always nylon, occasionally reinforced with leather or heavy Cordura®.

Fanny packs attach using a strap around your waist and always fasten in front. Usually constructed of nylon, they have zippers, several compartments and snap-together buckles for easy removal. Small fanny packs are worn for keeping makeup or change in and are 400 cubic inches in size. Larger, padded packs, which will hold a day's supplies, are compartmentalized and have outside straps for carrying additional articles.

Internal Frame Packs

Internal frame packs are larger than day packs and are used for activities that require more gear and more than 20 pounds of equipment. They have a frame that ties into a waist belt system, which supports a majority of the load. They are good for ski touring, snowshoeing, winter mountaineering, technical climbing and backpacking.

The main reason for choosing an internal frame pack over an external frame pack is that it sits directly against your back. For activities done in rough terrain, requiring extremes in range of motion, the internal frame pack hugs your body, keeping the center of gravity close to you. As a result, this type of pack is warmer during hot weather than the external frame pack because it fits so close to your body.

Features to look for include: contoured padded shoulder straps, a sternum strap, well-padded hip belt, load compression straps, separate sleeping bag compartment and durable reinforced construction.

External Frame Packs

For overnight and extended trips on established trails, an external frame pack with a heavy-duty frame and sturdy, full-size bag is the wisest choice. Such packs provide a broader base of support, allowing for more variance in weight distribution and making it possible to carry heavy loads in an upright position, with most of the weight being supported by your hips. They are cooler because they don't press against your body.

External frame packs are usually half the price of an internal frame pack. They should have a lightweight aluminum tubing welded frame, a generously padded hip belt and shoulder straps. Ideally, they should have a sternum strap and load lifter straps.

There are usually six to eight outside compartments for separating your gear and making it easier to access. A good pack allows adjustment of both frame and bag to provide the correct fit for each individual. The bag should be attached to the frame with clevis pins and locking wire, not with flimsy cord loops sewn to the bag.

Packing a Backpack

There are three important considerations in packing a backpack: (1) organizing equipment, (2) providing easy access to important articles and (3) distributing the load for maximum comfort and efficiency.

Organization and Accessibility

Nylon ditty bags or plastic sacks are helpful for keeping gear organized and providing extra protection from water that may leak through the pack bag. Bags also keep the gear compact, making it easier to pack.

Everyone eventually works out a system of arranging gear, keeping important items such as rain gear and some food and necessary clothing within easy reach. In inclement weather, it's convenient to have the tent ready for unpacking first and repacking last.

Weight Distribution

The most important consideration in packing is centering the load over your vertical walking axis or center of gravity. The design of the pack helps greatly in centering the weight, but bad packing can keep any pack from riding correctly.

Avoid weighing down the lower portion of the pack. Too much weight too low will cause an unnatural pull on your back and strain both your back and leg muscles. When the load is correctly centered, it will normally ride fairly high on your back.

In loading your pack for on-trail hiking, pack heavy items higher and closer to your back, lighter items lower and farther away from your back, and the sleeping bag at the bottom. If you're hiking off the trail, pack lighter items higher and farther from your back, heavier items lower and closer to your back, and the sleeping bag at the top. The weight distribution will also vary according to what you are doing — hiking, skiing or climbing.

Pack frequently used gear, such as water bottles, in the most accessible places, such as near pack openings or in outside pockets. Lash long items, such as tent poles, sleeping pads or snow pickets, onto the sides of your pack, under the compression straps.

Hoisting the Pack

Putting on a heavy pack is not as easy as it might seem (Figures 12-1 to 12-4). You should develop a system for hoisting a pack

Figure 12-1. Pack resting on your knee

Figure 12-2. Putting your arm through the shoulder strap

Figure 12-3. Securing the pack onto your back

Figure 12-4. Cinching waist belt over hips

Figure 12-5. Pack in line

without help from another person or without even a rock to balance it on. Using your knee or bent leg as a support will help. Swing the pack onto your leg and rest it there while you put one arm through the shoulder strap. Then lean forward and push with your bent leg, swinging the pack onto your back and putting your other arm and both shoulders through and into position in a continuous motion.

With the pack resting on your shoulders, lean forward again, hunch your shoulders, and slide the pack up your back so you can cinch the padded waist belt securely over your hips. When you stand straight, the weight should fall naturally onto your hips. Be sure the shoulder straps are tight enough to keep the pack in line and the weight close to your back (Figure 12-5).

Lightweight Stoves

The lightweight stove has become one of the backpacker's most important pieces of equipment. With the increasing numbers of enthusiasts taking to the outdoors, firewood has grown scarce in many areas, and natural beauty has suffered with the removal of timber and picturesque snags. In many wilderness areas, campfires are prohibited, and much of the alpine terrain so popular with hikers is naturally limited in timber growth. What does survive the rigorous climates at high elevations is vital to the ecology and scenic value of the area. Open, meadow-covered areas are extremely fragile, and the black, charred remains of old fire pits are a blemish to the beauty of the wilderness.

There are a great variety of stoves on the market, and it can be a confusing task to select the one most suited to the kinds of trips you will be taking. Most of the lightweight stoves have one burner and weigh from 1 to 2 pounds. Consider such factors as climatic conditions, terrain, duration of the trip, distance to be traveled, number of people in the party, availability of water and the kinds of foods to be cooked. No stove will meet all conditions, so be prepared to compromise.

Stoves are generally classified under the type of fuel being used. The most common fuels are kerosene, propane/butane (cartridge), and white gas/multi-fuel.

Kerosene Stoves

The kerosene stove requires both pumping and priming, but it is a relatively efficient fuel as it burns. Kerosene is a reasonably safe, explosion-proof fuel, though it is somewhat messy because of its oily nature and slow evaporation. Kerosene is also a relatively inexpensive fuel and is one of several fuel options in the United States; however, it is often the only readily available fuel in many other countries.

Propane and Butane (Cartridge) Stoves

Propane comes in relatively heavy containers because of the high pressure needed to liquefy the gas, and while it is an excellent fuel, it is more often used in car camping than in backpacking because of the weight.

Butane stoves are popular with backpackers because of their simplicity and light weight. The gas comes in disposable cartridges that attach to the stove unit. The stoves do not require pumping or priming and provide an effective heat source that can be regulated from a full boil down to a fine simmer.

Virtually all butane stoves now have a mixture of propane in them to allow them to burn effectively in temperatures as low as 20° F.

Butane stoves are generally less expensive than gasoline stoves, but the cost of the fuel itself is much higher.

White Gas/Multi-Fuel

The type of gasoline most commonly used in outdoor stoves is a highly refined form of white gas called stove or lantern fuel. Coleman® fuel is a popular example. The many varieties of gas stoves range from small, lightweight models to bigger, heavier versions designed for maximum heat output. All need to be primed, and some utilize a pump. Gas stoves are usually a bit heavier than butane stoves, but the models designed for backpacking fall well within the acceptable weight limit.

A separate bottle of fuel must be carried for refilling the stove. Gas stoves offer an efficient heat source under many conditions, but they run hotter than butane stoves and are not as good for simmering. Also, gas stoves are somewhat more expensive than butane stoves, but the fuel is cheaper.

For winter camping, stoves with a pump work best and some

of the higher-powered gas stoves function well even in extremely cold temperatures.

Increasing the Effectiveness of Your Stove

The performance of any stove can be greatly increased by intelligent operation. Wind and cold can drastically reduce the efficiency of any stove, and the successful backpacker must know how to minimize the adverse effects of these two elements. Most stoves come with their own built-in or attachable wind protection devices, some more successful than others. To increase your stove's efficiency, select a sheltered place for operation, construct additional windbreaks and keep fuel bottles, cartridges and stoves out of the cold by wrapping them in clothing or storing them in sleeping bags overnight.

Safety and Care of Stoves

Intelligent use and care of your stove not only helps prevent broken parts while in the wilderness, but may also avert a serious accident.

- Take care not to overheat any stove, particularly one using butane or gasoline.
- When insulating the stove from the wind and cold, be sure you don't cut off the oxygen supply to the stove or create an oven-like effect, thereby baking the stove in its own heat.
- Avoid operating the stove in a closely confined area, such as a tent, and don't pile dirt or rocks too closely around it.
- Use small pots and pans to avoid reflecting too much heat back onto the stove.
- Keep the stove and fuel containers away from other sources of heat.
- Butane is highly flammable and care must be taken when changing cartridges. Be sure that all the gas is used up before removing the cartridge.
- Gasoline stoves must be primed carefully. The most popular primers are alcohol or a fuel paste. Avoid drenching the priming cup with too much fuel; only a small amount is needed.
- Know the construction and operation of your stove thoroughly, so you can both prevent and identify malfunctions.
- Inspect and clean your stove frequently, replacing worn-out or damaged parts.

Cooking Equipment

Simplicity and multi-use are the key words in selecting cooking equipment. Take only what is needed, and then use your imagination to concoct a varied menu with limited equipment.

Pots and Pans

If your party is limited to two or three persons, often a 2- or 3-quart pot with a lid is sufficient. The lid can serve as a pan for frying or as an extra plate. For larger parties, choose a set of pots, pans and plates of various sizes that nest together into one compact unit. Some pot-and-pan kits dispense with handles to save space. In this case, a potholder is a necessary implement.

Most lightweight campers prefer stainless steel cookware because of the health concerns of cooking in aluminum. All utensils should be either stainless steel, Lexan® (plastic) or aluminum.

All-Purpose Cup

A stainless steel cup is an indispensable tool. It can be used to hold hot and cold liquids, cereals, soups, stews, puddings and so on. It can even serve as a pot in which to cook or as a plate for portions of a main course. The cup can also be a handy tool for measuring.

Be sure to buy a cup with a heat-resistant handle. If you want a deeper cup, there are several insulated, unbreakable plastic cups on the market.

Water Bottle

Polycarbonate bottles are the best choice. They are lightweight, durable, clear and do not retain odors. Wide-mouth bottles are easier to clean and use for mixing.

Utensils

You'll need a lightweight stainless steel knife-fork-spoon set that nests together. Also include a can opener and a good pocketknife.

Miscellaneous Items

Plastic or nylon "ditty" bags are excellent to compartmentalize food, small items, and cooking and eating equipment. A spill-proof combination salt and pepper shaker is useful. All kinds of other culinary gadgets can be purchased, many of which are convenient but not really necessary.

Backpacking Tents

The hiker's continual exposure to potentially severe weather conditions makes shelter a very important consideration. As a backpacker, you're on your own, away from civilization, roads and facilities. If the weather turns bad, you'll have to accept it and be prepared to cope with it; you can't climb into your car and head for the warmth of your home. Careful selections made from a specialized line of equipment will ensure adequate shelter.

Capacity

The lightweight camper must make do with a minimum of room. A shelter will have much less space than a tent used for car camping with a corresponding number of people. Backpacking or three-season tents usually range from a one-person to four-person capacity, the most popular being for two and three persons.

Many tents feature a vestibule—an extension of the main body of the tent—in which gear can be stowed. If you will be spending a lot of time in the tent, or if you simply prefer more room, choose a larger tent.

Weight and Bulk

As a lightweight camper, you'll carry your shelter on your back, so you'll be less concerned with capacity than with ease of transport. Emphasis is on maximum protection and durability with a minimum of weight and bulk. One- to two-person tents usually range anywhere from 3 to 8 pounds. Three- and four-person tents weigh from 9 to 12 pounds.

Ease of Assembly

You'll need a tent that is simply put together, with a minimum of parts. Camp is often set up in windy, cold and wet weather. At such times you'll appreciate a tent that is pitched easily, with no complications or frustrating obstacles. Ease in setting up and breaking camp is also desirable; backpackers tend to move their camps frequently.

Materials and Construction

Most lightweight tents are made of tightly woven, ripstop nylon and nylon taffeta. Nylon is durable, lightweight, compacts well and is easily packed.

Figure 12-6. Rain-fly

The tent should also have a coated nylon rain-fly. The rain-fly (Figure 12-6) will help keep the inner tent dry in foul weather, and it will help reduce condensation if it is properly fitted to the tent. Poles are usually made of aluminum and shock corded to speed assembly.

Tent Care

Your tent should be kept dry whenever possible. Be sure your tent is completely dry and aired before storing it for more than a day or two. At home, store the tent in a dry, cool place, rolled up loosely in a box or bag. Keep it out of the sun since sunlight (ultraviolet rays) tends to weaken nylon in time.

Keeping your tent clean will prolong its life. Grit and dirt not only contribute to discomfort, they can seriously wear away at the delicate materials of your tent. Always clean your tent when your trip is over, shaking it out and wiping it or washing it by hand.

Emergency Shelters

Emergency shelters are lightweight alternatives to tents. If your concern is not so much durability and comfort as it is economy, and if you're traveling in good weather and want a quick, conve-

Figure 12-7. Makeshift tarp

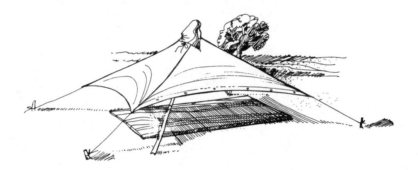

Figure 12-8. Poncho

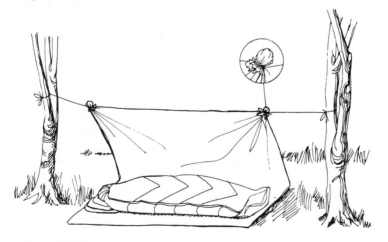

Figure 12-9. Groundsheet

nient shelter for the night, carry along a tarp (Figure 12-7). Always have enough rope to secure the tarp. Trees are often not in the right locations, so you might consider taking poles.

Ponchos can double as a walking protection against the weather and as a small tent if you carry poles, pegs and lines (Figure 12-8).

A large, plastic grommeted groundsheet can act as a ground protection and an angled roof at the same time. Not very durable, stones and sharp twigs may puncture it. Don't plan to keep it long (Figure 12-9).

Accessories

It's a good idea to carry along a lightweight tarp or groundsheet, slightly smaller than the floor of the tent, to put under your tent. Tent floors on most backpacking tents are very lightweight and thin. The tarp will assist in keeping out moisture and will help protect the floor, adding life to the tent.

Lightweight Sleeping Bags

Sleeping gear is very important if you are a backpacker because you are exposed to extremes in weather. Weight is crucial; your bag must have maximum warmth with a minimum of bulk and weight. Choose a bag that will meet the requirements for your outing. Most sleeping bags are rated for warmth by the manufacturer, but these ratings are very general and may not apply in every case because of the great variability in individual metabolism.

In selecting the right bag, determine if you are going to use it for three or four seasons. If you're going to use it primarily during the spring, summer and fall, a bag with a temperature rating of + 20° F will be adequate for the average person. If you have a lower metabolism and become cold easily, a temperature rating of + 10° F or even 0° F may be preferred.

If you plan to use your bag during the winter and will be digging a snow cave, the three-season bag will probably suffice. For winter tent camping, select a bag rated to the coldest temperature you anticipate being in.

No one sleeping bag is ideal for all purposes. Weather, metabolism, clothing, ground insulation, shelter and bag construction will all determine the degree of warmth and comfort of the bag.

If you decide on a summer bag, you'll need to choose between down or synthetic. A synthetic bag will keep you warm even if it gets wet. It can be totally soaked, but you can wring it out and the bag will be dry before you wake in the morning. Down bags can take up to a week to dry.

In order to stay warm in subfreezing temperatures, a synthetic bag would have to be heavy and bulky. Down is compact and lightweight, the best choice for winter campers.

Since heat is not produced by the sleeping bag, the purpose of the fill is to retain the heat produced by the body. The fill creates dead air space (loft) and comfort range. The loft refers to the thickness of the insulation. The thicker the loft, the warmer the bag.

The shape of the bag is another consideration. A mummy bag is the warmest for it's shape, but not the best choice for someone who is claustrophobic. Semi-mummy bags have a little more room throughout the bag and are also large in volume. A semi-rectangular bag has a squared-off top without a hood. The foot area is tapered so that your feet don't have to heat up such a large area.

Your metabolism must also be considered when you are selecting a sleeping bag. If you have less body fat, you are more apt to become cold than if you have a comfortable excess. Being dehydrated or hungry will also add to your lack of body heat generation. Dressing warmly while you sleep by wearing some long underwear, a stocking cap and a pair of wool socks can compensate for some of these factors. Make sure no part of your body is constricted by your sleepwear.

Insulated Sleeping Bags

The down or fiber in your sleeping bag compresses under your weight and leaves very little thickness between you and the cold ground. The backpacker's favorite insulated sleeping pad is self-inflating and features a waterproof nylon cover bonded to warm, open-cell foam. Pads deflate for easy packing.

Food for Lightweight Camping

Being creative in planning and cooking lightweight meals out-of-doors can be wonderfully rewarding—or frustrating and expensive if you don't have the know-how. For excellent eating on the trail, I recommend using a combination of supermarket foods, some fresh foods that travel well (depending on the length and the weight allowance of the trip), and home-dried foods.

If you give the necessary time and thought to planning, you can eat like a king on the trail! Here are some handy tips.

Meal Planning

Well-planned, nutritious meals are a must for the backpacker, not only to keep energy levels high, but also to keep spirits high. Good food is always a principal ingredient of good times.

The Food Pyramid

The basics of good meal planning apply on the trail as well as at home. Try to plan your daily meals around the Food Pyramid discussed in chapter six, including the following: four or more servings of fruits and vegetables, six or more of breads and cereals, two servings of dairy products, and two servings from the meat group including other protein sources such as legumes and nuts.

Bulk and Weight

Since bulk and weight are important considerations in lightweight camping, take foods that have the highest caloric and nutritional value for their respective weight and bulk. Foods high in carbohydrates and fats are proportionately higher in calories.

General Meal Planning Suggestions

Plan simple breakfasts with a hot cereal or drink on cold mornings, lunches that can be eaten along the way, and dinners with one hot dish. In creating daily menus, plan for:

- Variety (a steady diet of anything gets old pretty fast)
- Flavor (some foods spicy, some bland)
- Texture (crunchy, soft, chewy)
- Temperature (hot, cold)
- Color (food that looks good somehow always tastes better)

Packaging

Food should be premeasured and repacked for daily use. Depending on the length of the trip and individual preference, compartmentalize food according to "trail food," "breakfasts," "dinners" and "foods to be cooked."

Reduce bulk wherever possible by squeezing excess air out of plastic bags. Home vacuum packaging appliances carry pouches that are airtight, moisture-proof and strong. They can also be used in boiling water, which eliminates messy clean-up.

On the Trail

Here are some food tips while on the trail:

Reconstituting Dehydrated Foods

Add water to dehydrated vegetables in a heavy-duty freezer bag during a lunch break. Remove the air and seal the bag. For added protection, place it in another sealed bag. The food will be reconstituted by meal-preparation time. Home-dried foods take longer to reconstitute than freeze-dried foods.

Drinking Water

Keep a folded plastic bag in your pocket. When you find a source of clean water, fill the bag and add a water purification tablet. When the bag is empty, zip it, fold it and place it in your pocket again for the next use. Portable water purification devices are also available. Prices vary depending on the contaminants they remove.

Mixing Food

Mix foods such as cake mixes, pancake mix, meat loaf and others in heavy, self-sealing plastic bags. Place the item to be mixed in the plastic bag, set the bag on a flat surface, and with your hands on each side of the bag, move them to the top of the bag, forcing out excess air. Zip the bag shut and, holding the bag in one hand, squeeze the food with the other until properly mixed.

Setting Jell-O

Following the directions on the package, dissolve Jell-O in water. Place the mixture in a self-sealing plastic bag and remove as much air as possible. Seal it and set it in a cool place, such as a stream. To form the Jell-O, place the bag inside a #10 can.

No-Cook Recipes

Here are three "goodies" you might make without lighting a fire.

PEANUT BUTTER BALLS

- Combine in large, self-sealing
  plastic bag   ½ cup peanut butter

  ½ cup dry milk powder

- Add and mix   ½ cup honey

  1 tablespoon carob or cocoa
      powder

- Add and mix   ¼ cup chopped nuts

  ¼ cup raisins

  ¼ cup chopped dates

  2 tablespoons coconut

After cleaning hands, lightly coat with vegetable oil. Roll mixture
with hands into 1-inch balls. Store in plastic wrap.

WALKING SALAD

- Cut around the top and remove core
  and seeds from   1 apple

- Add   raisins mixed with 1 to 2
      tablespoons chunky
      peanut butter

Fill the apple cavity with peanut butter mixture. This is a refreshing
snack and provides quick energy on hikes. You might want to put
the apple in a plastic bag to eat as a snack on the trail.

ORANGE-WITH-PEPPERMINT-STRAW DRINK

- On a hard surface, squeeze
  and roll to loosen juice of   1 orange

With a pocketknife or other slim, sharp blade, cut out one end of
the orange, leaving a small hole (⅜-inch in diameter). Slide the knife
blade down into the hole and cut the meat in several places to release
the juice.

- Into the hole insert one end of   1 peppermint stick (or
      porous candy)

Suck on the other end of the peppermint stick as you would a straw.
The orange juice will come up through the peppermint stick.
Squeeze the orange periodically to release the juice.

Supermarket Convenience Foods

Supermarkets carry a wide variety of dried convenience foods. Quality, price and brand vary from store to store, but by checking the ingredients, weight and price, you can make comparisons to get the most for your money. Before buying, check to see what items need to be added to mixes (such as hamburger or eggs) to make sure they are practical for your trip.

Store brands are generally 5 to 20 percent less expensive than name brands and often as good in quality. Buying larger quantities is, generally, less expensive.

Supermarket mixes such as pancake or biscuit mix are usually about half as expensive as the ones found in backpacking supply stores. If you have the time, you can again cut the price in half by making your own. The following prepared foods are ideal for lightweight camping.

Trail Foods

These are foods to eat on the trail when you don't want to bother building a fire or lighting a stove, or when you just need an energy lift. They can be used to supplement meals.

Dried Fruits

Apples (with variations—cinnamon, strawberry, etc.)
Apricots
Banana chips
Blueberries
Cherries
Dates
Figs
Fruit rolls and fruit leather
Fruit-and-nut combinations
Mangoes
Papaya
Peaches
Pears
Pineapple
Prunes
Raisins

Protein Foods

Cheese
  hard
  processed cheese snacks
Fish, canned
Instant breakfast
Jerky
Meats, canned
Meat sticks
Nuts
Peanut butter

Breads and Cereals

Bread sticks

Cookies (bar type), such as fig bars

Crackers that don't crumble easily

Roman Meal®

Ry-Krisp®

Triscuits®

English muffins

French or sourdough breads

Granola

Granola bars

Melba Toast®

Pita bread

Pop Tarts®

Rye bread

Tortillas

Whole grain breads

Candies

(Anything that doesn't melt or mash easily)

Hard candies

Gumdrops

Jelly beans

Staples

Flour

Honey

Jam

Margarine or butter

Peanut butter

Powdered milk

Salt and pepper

Spices

Sugar

 brown (brown sugar + water = syrup)

 granulated

Vegetable oil

Breakfast Foods

Bacon bits

Bacon, canned, sliced

Bisquick®

Breads, whole grain

Breakfast squares, fortified

Cereals, hot, instant

Cornbread mix

Dried fruits

French toast mix

Granola

Granola bars

Hash browns, dried

Meat sticks

Muffin and scone mixes

Pancake mix, complete

Soups and Stews

Chili

Noodles, "instant Oriental" and base

Soup, instant

Stew base mixes including bouillon—instant or cubes

Gravy mixes

Powdered stock base mixes

Meats and Other Proteins

Chipped beef
Deviled ham
Lunchmeat
Spam®
Vienna Sausage®

Fish, beef or chicken (canned)
Jerky
Meat sticks
Salami (dry)
Vegetable protein, texturized

Main Dishes

(Add dehydrated hamburger
  or T.V.P. – Textured
  Vegetable Protein)
Hamburger Helper® type
  Beef noodle
  Cheeseburger noodle
  Chili-tomato
  Hamburger stew
  Lasagne
  Potato stroganoff
  Rice
  Spaghetti

Tuna Helper® type (add tuna,
  ham, chicken or turkey
  chunks)
Creamy noodles with
  vegetables
Creamy rice
Newburg
Noodles and cheese sauce

Side Dishes

(Some may be adapted to
  main-course dinners)
Gravy mixes
Macaroni and cheese
Macaroni salad mixes
Mushrooms, sliced,
  dehydrated
Noodle mixes
Potatoes, dehydrated
  Flakes
  Powdered
  Shredded
  Sliced

Potato mixes
  Au gratin
  Scalloped
Rice, instant, precooked
Rice mixes (Rice-a-Roni®
  types)
Sauce mixes (sour cream,
  white sauce, teriyaki,
  sweet 'n' sour)
Tuna salad mixes
Vegetable flakes

Desserts

Cake mixes requiring only
  water
Cheesecake, instant
Danish dessert mix
Fruit cobblers
Fruit dumplings

Jell-O
Popcorn
Pudding, instant
Pudding snacks, canned
  (bulky but easy)

Beverages

Breakfast drinks, powdered,
  fruit-flavored
    Grape
    Grapefruit
    Orange
    Tomato
Cocoa mix, hot

Coffee
Drinks (Kool-Aid® type),
  powdered, fruit-flavored
    Artificially sweetened
    Presweetened with sugar
Milk, instant, dry
Tea

Fresh Foods That Travel Well

If space and weight allow, there are a number of fresh foods that keep well without refrigeration for four or five days. Use the fresh foods on the first couple of days of the trip, which means a lighter pack later. The following suggestions should help you to keep the food in top condition:

- Pack only fresh, unbruised, top-quality fruits and vegetables.
- Do not wash fruit and vegetables before packing; it will cause them to deteriorate more rapidly.
- For better insulation, pack foods that should be kept cooler in the center of your pack.
- Pack foods that crush or bruise more easily in side pockets or in cooking pots.
- Pack each fruit or vegetable in a brown paper bag to retain freshness.
- When carrying fresh meat (usually for use on the first day), freeze the meat solid, slit the plastic store wrapper, wrap the meat in newspapers to insulate, and place the whole package in a brown paper bag.

Fruits

Apples

Citrus fruits

Melons

Vegetables

Beans	Parsnips
Broccoli	Peas
Carrots	Peppers
Celery	Potatoes
Cucumbers	Sprouts
Garlic	Turnips
Mushrooms	Zucchini
Onions	

Freeze-Dried Foods

Freeze-dried, prepackaged meals need no special preparation, are usually three to six times more expensive than comparable supermarket or home-dried items, and are frequently not as tasty. The only exception to this is meat — hamburger, in particular. You may choose to buy freeze-dried meats or hamburger to add to supermarket main-dish mixes.

Drying Your Own Foods

It's easy and fun to dry your own foods with a home food dehydrator. Drying foods at home is becoming more and more popular as a means of preservation for general home use as well as for lightweight camping.

There are many advantages to drying your own foods. Dried foods occupy from one-fifth to one-twentieth of the storage space and weight of canned or frozen foods. When properly stored, most dried foods keep for at least a year, retaining top quality and nutritional value. There is no danger of botulism with dehydrated foods. As with other methods of preservation, drying in season is a tremendous money-saver, adding interesting variety to home food stores and snacks.

The drying process is quite simple. Sliced or cut foods are placed on racks, which allow air to circulate around the food. The moisture slowly evaporates because of an elevated temperature, and the circulating air removes the moisture.

Sun-Drying

If you live in the Southwest or a warm climate where you can count on five or more days of continuous sunshine, low humidity and temperatures about 90° F daily, you might want to try nature's way of preserving foods. Sun-drying is the most time-consuming and least expensive method of food preservation.

Place foods to be dried on screens (polypropolene or nylon-coated fiber glass) and find the warmest, sunniest and safest spot in your yard. By safest, I mean a place where the neighborhood dogs, cats or children won't nibble up your goodies before they dry. Place the food as far away from dust, roads and exhaust as possible. To protect it from birds and insects, cover it with cheesecloth or nylon netting — propped up so it doesn't touch the food.

Be sure that the location has good air circulation, and if you choose to stack the screens after the food has partially dried, rotate them from top to bottom two or three times each day. Occasionally turning the fruit facilitates even drying. Stacking the screens during the last half of the drying process produces a nicer flavor and color because the food is less exposed to direct sunlight.

The food should be brought in at night or at the first sign of rain, because moisture on partially dried food will cause it to mildew and spoil.

Oven Drying

Oven drying tends to produce lower-quality dried foods because it is difficult to maintain a temperature below 140° F unless your oven is specifically designed to do so. Most convection ovens work quite well for drying because they have a fan that circulates the air and removes moisture. Since ovens vary in their range of temperature, size and efficiency, experiment with yours to see what produces the best results. Make sure that your oven will maintain a temperature of 140° F or below before attempting to dry in it.

Make a pillowcase-type covering out of nylon net to fit snugly over each oven rack so food can be dried on the net without falling through. If you want to dry larger quantities, try obtaining a couple of extra oven racks (frequently available from used appliance dealers) to make the most of your energy and the oven's. An average oven rack has about 2½ square feet, so with four racks, the total drying area would be about 10 square feet.

Load the racks with the food to be dried, leaving space between the foods for adequate air circulation. Don't overlap food on the trays. This results in unevenly dried food and longer drying times.

If your oven does not have a convection feature, set it to the lowest setting (ideally between 125° and 140° F) and crack the door about ½ to 1 inch in an electric oven or 8 inches in a gas oven by inserting a lid near the door hinge. Check the oven temperature on each rack with an oven thermometer and adjust accordingly. In some gas ovens, the pilot light keeps the oven warm enough. If your gas oven does not have an automatic shut-off valve, check it occasionally to make sure the flame is still on.

Rotate racks every 2 to 3 hours for the most even drying. Cool the foods before you check them for dryness.

Dehydrators

A wide variety of consumer dehydrators are available in stores or through catalogs or TV ads. Take the time to compare different dehydrators to make sure you buy the most efficient one, and one that will best suit your needs.

Round, stackable units with a fan, heating element and thermostat are ideal because they are expandable. Beware of ones that only contain a heating element. They take considerably longer to dry than those with a fan, and seldom have temperatures above 120° F, which is too low for meats, poultry or low-acid foods. Most round, stackable dryers with a fan and thermostat do not need to be rotated because the design allows for even airflow.

Box dryers also work very well. The only limitations are the lack of expandability and the need to occasionally rotate the trays.

Making your own dehydrator is impractical due to the availability and reasonable prices of consumer dehydrators on the market. Dryers made from wood are unsafe due to their flammability. They are also difficult to clean and use far more electricity than metal and plastic manufactured ones.

Safety features should include U.L. approval, nonflammable

construction, enclosed electrical components and a safety switch in case of thermostat failure.

The cost of operation depends on the wattage of the heating element. If a portion of the air recirculates within the dryer and the heating element is thermostatically controlled, the cost of operation will be lower.

Check for the location of the closest dealer and service. Also check for length of warranty and what it covers, shipping costs if the dryer needs to be returned to the manufacturer for repairs, and how easily parts can be replaced after the warranty has expired.

Drying Fruits

Dried fruits are an ideal source of concentrated quick energy — usually eaten as they are. They can also be used in cookies and other baked goods, puddings and fruit salads. Dried fruits weigh anywhere from one-fourth to one-twentieth of their fresh or canned weight.

Only fresh, ripe fruits should be dried. Discard any bruised or overripe fruit. Allow underripe fruit to ripen. Fruits such as apricots or peaches do not ripen once they are picked. They soften and change color, but don't get sweeter or more flavorful. Tree-ripened fruit is the best for drying and eating. Wash and handle the fruit carefully. Soaking fruits that brown in ascorbic acid solutions prevents oxidative browning during preparation.

Fruits to be dried may be categorized in three groups:

1. *Slice and dry (bananas, pineapple, etc.).* Remove inedible peelings and slice most fruits ¼- to ⅛-inch thick. Slice evenly if possible. Evenly sliced rounds dry more quickly than wedges.
2. *Fruits with edible skins (cherries, prunes, grapes, blueberries).* Fruits with skins dry more quickly if the skins are broken by halving, pitting, freezing or dipping in boiling water until the skins crack. Freezing is preferred over boiling water, but they tend to drip during drying. Place on trays with skin side down to prevent dripping.
3. *Fruits that oxidize (apples, pears, peaches, apricots).* Fruits that oxidize darken when they are cut and exposed to the air. They also lose their flavor as well as vitamins A and C during drying

DRYING CHART FOR FRUIT

Fruit	Preparation for Drying	Dryness Test	Fruit Rolls	Backpacking Suggestions
Slice and Dry				
Bananas	Slice ¾-inch or divide lengthwise into thirds by pressing thumb into stem end. Riper bananas will turn darker and have a stronger flavor.	Leathery to crisp	Combines nicely with pineapple.	Dip in dry Jell-O, honey/lemon juice mixture and then in sesame seeds, chopped nuts or melted chocolate.
Coconut	Crack shell, drain milk and steam meat 30 seconds to loosen from shell; peel, grate and dry at 110° F.	Leathery	May be sprinkled on fruit leathers as a garnish, but leather must then be stored in the freezer.	To sweeten: shake coconut in powdered sugar prior to drying. Use in fruit balls and granola.
Oranges	Slice in ¾-inch rings with peel.	Crisp	Only in combination with other fruits.	Peel may be eaten.
Pineapple	Pare, core and slice in ½-inch rings.	Leathery	Combines well with apricot or canned fruit to add fresh flavor.	Good in trail mix or gorp.
Rhubarb	Wash, slice in 1-inch pieces and steam until hot.	Crisp	Combine with strawberry purée and sweeten with corn syrup or honey.	Best in fruit leather.
Strawberries	Wash, remove stems, and slice in half.	Leathery to crisp	Purée in blender.	Sprinkle with strawberry Jell-O for a "candied" strawberry.
Fruits With Edible Skins				
Berries	Raspberries, boysenberries and blackberries are best in leathers. Too seedy to dry alone.		Purée and sieve to remove part of seeds. Add 2 teaspoons powdered pectin per quart of purée. Warm to bath temperature, or mix with apple purée for leather without added pectin.	Leather is good in fruit balls or trail mix.
Cherries	Wash and pit or halve.	Leathery	Add ½ teaspoon almond extract per 2 cups purée and a pinch of sodium bisulfite. Combine with raspberries, apples or pineapple.	Eat like raisins or in trail mix.

Roughing It Easy

DRYING CHART FOR FRUIT

Fruit	Preparation for Drying	Dryness Test	Fruit Rolls	Backpacking Suggestions
Slice and Dry				
Dates	Pit, slice lengthwise, or cube in ½-inch cubes. May be rolled in lemon juice and then in granulated or brown sugar prior to drying.	Leathery to very firm	May be used as a natural sweetening in other fruit leathers.	Use date filling to "sandwich" together two sheets of apricot leather. Date filling: cook 8 ounces dates, ½ cup sugar, ½ cup water, and 1 teaspoon lemon juice until thickened.
Grapes	Wash. Use only seedless grapes.	Leathery	Purée. Sweeten with honey or white corn syrup. Combines nicely with apples.	Great additions to trail mix and cereals.
Plums and Prunes	Wash and halve. Remove pits. Dry skin side down. May be sulfured to increase shelf life and keep color light.	Leathery	Wash, pit and purée. If very runny, add 2 teaspoons pectin and warm. Combines nicely with apples.	Sprinkle with Jell-O for different flavor.
Fruits That Oxidize				
Apples	Pare, core and slice in ¼-inch rings. Crisp, tart varieties dry best. Sulfur or soak in sulfite solution.	Leathery to crisp	Pare, core, cook until soft; purée. May add cinnamon, nutmeg or red cinnamon candies. May use canned applesauce.	Chop dry apples in blender to make "instant" applesauce mix. Sprinkle apple slices with Jell-O or cinnamon-sugar mixture before drying.
Apricots	Wash, halve and remove pits. Sulfuring preferred. May be syrup blanched for a candied apricot.	Leathery	Pit, purée and add pinch of sodium bisulfite. Combines well with pineapple.	Add small pieces to main dishes or desserts.
Peaches or Nectarines	Wash, blanch, cool, peel and remove pits. Slice ½-inch crosswise. Sulfur or soak in sulfite solution.	Leathery	Purée and add pinch of sodium bisulfite. Combines nicely with fresh pineapple (1 part pineapple purée to 3 parts peach).	Good in trail mix.
Pears	Wash, pare, core and slice lengthwise in ½-inch slices. Sulfur or soak in sulfite solution.	Leathery	Purée and add pinch of sodium bisulfite. Combines nicely with apples.	Good in trail mix.

and storage if they are not pretreated by one of the methods listed below (in order of preference).

Sulfuring

Sulfuring must be done outdoors with good ventilation and is the best method for preventing oxidation. Sulfur dioxide gas "seals" the surface area of the fruit, reducing loss of color, flavor and vitamins A and C. During the drying process, the sulfur dioxide oxidizes, leaving no harmful chemicals on the fruit. *A note of caution:* Sulfur dioxide fumes are dangerous to your lungs. Use sulfur in a well-ventilated area outside and do not breathe the fumes.

- Prepare the fruit. Hold it in ascorbic-acid solution (1 teaspoon per ½ gallon of water) while preparing it for pretreatment.
- Place the fruit on trays (wood, nylon or fiberglass) and stack the trays 2 inches apart, using a rack or wooden blocks.
- Place the flowers of sulfur (sublimed sulfur) in a clean, shallow pan in front of the trays of fruit. (Use 1 teaspoon of sulfur per 2 pounds of prepared fruit.) Make sure you have at least 10 inches in front of the trays for the sulfur pan.
- Cover the stacked trays with a large cardboard box with 4 × 4-inch flaps cut in the lower front and top back.
- Pack the lower edges of the box with sand.
- Open the flaps and ignite the sulfur. Burn it until the sulfur is almost consumed; then close the flaps.
- Let the fruit stand in the sulfur box 30 minutes to 1 hour for thin slices, 1 to 1½ hours for halved fruit.
- Immediately place the fruit in the dryer. The dryer should be outside in a well-ventilated area for the first several hours.

Sulfiting

Soaking fruit in a solution of sodium bisulfite produces results similar to sulfuring in apples, peaches and pears. Sodium bisulfite is available from winemaking supply stores or drugstores. *A note of caution:* Avoid sulfiting fruit if you have asthma or any respiratory disorders.

- Slice the fruit directly into a colander submerged in a holding solution of 1 teaspoon ascorbic acid per ½ gallon of water.
- Remove colander and soak the fruit for 5 to 10 minutes in a sodium bisulfite solution (1 tablespoon per gallon of water).

- Remove the colander from the sulfite solution. Rinse under running cold water and immediately place the fruit on dryer trays.

Syrup Blanching
If you prefer not to use sulfur or sulfite, syrup blanching produces a "candied" kind of dried fruit. Simmer the prepared fruit for 10 minutes in a solution containing 1 cup of white corn syrup, 1½ cups of sugar and 3 cups of water. Then remove the fruit, rinse it in clear water, drain and place it in the dryer.

Dryness Test
Most fruits should be dried until they are pliable and leathery, with no pockets of moisture. Take a piece out of the dryer, allow it to cool and feel it. Monitor it closely when foods are nearly dried, and remove those pieces that are sufficiently dry. Over-dried fruit is hard, tough, tasteless and loses most nutrients.

Apples may be dried until they are crisp without damaging the fruit or lessening the nutritive value. They remain in better condition during storage if they are crisp rather than leathery.

Pasteurlzation
If a fruit is dried with the skins intact, microscopic insect larvae may remain on the skins even though they are thoroughly washed. To make sure you won't have problems later on, fruits with skins should be pasteurized by placing the packaged fruit in the freezer for at least 24 hours. Freezing kills all traces of insect larvae.

Storage
With the availability of home vacuum packaging devices such as the Foodsaver™, it is possible to dramatically increase the shelf life of dried foods. Dried fruits that are vacuum packaged in Foodsaver bags will last three to four times longer than fruits stored in freezer bags.

The length of time you can store dried foods is dependent upon exposure to heat, light and air. The ideal is vacuum packaging, then storage in the freezer or refrigerator. For every 18° F drop in temperature, the shelf life increases three to four times.

If you don't have access to a vacuum packager, package foods in self-sealing freezer bags, expelling as much air as possible.

Store them in the refrigerator or freezer or the coolest room in your house.

When properly packaged and stored below 60° F, most fruits will maintain good quality for at least one year. They keep much longer if vacuum packaged and/or stored in the freezer.

Fruit Leather

Another favorite among lightweight campers is fruit leather, a chewy fruit roll made by pulverizing fresh fruit in the blender and drying it to a leatherlike consistency. Instructions for specific fruit leather are included in the chart on fruits, but you'll find some general information below that may be helpful.

- Line the dryer trays with "fruit roll sheets" made by each dryer manufacturer especially for drying fruit rolls. Spray the trays lightly with vegetable spray or wipe them lightly with vegetable oil to prevent sticking. Do not use foil or waxed paper unless you want to eat it with your fruit leather!
- Purée the fresh fruit in the blender until it is a smooth, even consistency.
- Pour on sheets about ¼-inch thick, then tap the tray lightly to spread the pureé. Most fruits are delicious just as they are, but if the fresh fruit isn't fully ripe, try sweetening it with honey or white corn syrup. (Granulated sugar tends to crystallize during storage, resulting in brittle leather.) The purée will concentrate in sweetness as it dries. Artificial sweeteners may also be used. A small amount of lemon juice or ascorbic acid added to the purée tends to bring out the natural fruit flavor, and increases the vitamin C content of the fruit leather.
- Dry fruit leather until it is pliable but not sticky to the touch. Peel it off the drying sheet and roll like a jelly roll.
- Cut the leather roll into 4-inch pieces, wrap each piece individually in plastic wrap and label. (Many fruit leathers look alike.) Place the wrapped rolls in a moisture-proof container, self-sealing bag or Foodsaver™ bag for storage. Refrigerate, freeze or store in a cool, dark place.

Variations on Fruit Leather

1. *Canned fruit.* Canned fruit makes delicious leather. Drain the syrup and pureé the fruit in the blender. Many fruits combine

nicely with fresh pineapple, which adds a fresher flavor. Use one part fresh pineapple pureé to three parts canned fruit pureé.

2. *Leather pinwheels.* Spread a filling (see date filling under the chart on drying fruit, page 205) over the dried leather, rolling it and cutting it into pieces. Peanut butter and cream cheese can also be used. Eat immediately.

3. *Leather combinations.* Try rolling two or three different fruit leathers together and cutting them into pieces.

4. *"Crunchy" leathers.* Sprinkle chopped nuts, flaked coconut or granola over fruit leather and roll it. These are best if sprinkled on the pureé prior to drying. If it is kept longer than two weeks, store it in a freezer.

Drying Vegetables

Most vegetables dry well and retain most nutrients, color and flavor. Vegetables are scarce among commercially dehydrated foods and supermarket convenience foods. It's definitely an advantage to dry your own.

Preparation for Drying

With a few exceptions, vegetables need to be blanched prior to drying to inactivate enzymes that cause the food to deteriorate during drying and storage. Steam blanching is preferred over water blanching because it preserves more vitamins.

Since blanching time varies with altitude, thickness of vegetable slices and quantity blanched at one time, use the times listed in the following chart as a guideline. The vegetables should be partially cooked—tender to cut, but not quite done enough to eat.

If vegetables are not peeled, the skins are tough when rehydrated. You must make this choice based on your personal preference.

If you want to dry vegetables the easiest way possible, buy commercially frozen ones and simply place them on dryer trays and dry them. They have already been blanched for freezing, so no other preparation is necessary. It works great for beans, peas, corn, carrots and hash brown potatoes.

DRYING CHART FOR VEGETABLES

Vegetable	Preparation for Drying	Serving Suggestions
Green beans	Slice diagonally in 1-inch pieces or French cut. Steam blanch 2 to 4 minutes.	Soups, stews, cream of mushroom soup.
Beets	Cook or steam until tender. Cut in ¼-inch shoestring pieces.	Pickled beets; rehydrate with ½ cup water, ½ cup vinegar, 2 tablespoons sugar, ½ teaspoon salt, dash cloves, 1 bay leaf, 2 tablespoons onion flakes.
Cabbage	Shred in ¼-inch strips. Steam blanch 2 to 4 minutes.	Use in potato soup mix and stew.
Carrots	Peel, slice ¼-inch thick, and steam blanch 3 to 5 minutes. Remove and dip in a cornstarch solution of 2 tablespoons cornstarch to 2 cups water.	Soups, stews.
Celery	Slice diagonally ½-inch thick. Water blanch 30 seconds to 1 minute in a solution of ½ teaspoon baking soda to 1 cup water.	Soups, stews, powdered dry in blender for celery flakes or seasonings.
Chilies	Slice lengthwise or chop. Do not steam.	Powder dry in blender for chili.
Corn	Steam blanch on cob 3 to 4 minutes. Put in ice water. Cut from cob.	Rehydrate with 1 cup milk, 2 tablespoons sugar, ¼ teaspoon salt, enough water to cover.
Cucumbers	Slice ³/₁₆-inch thick and sprinkle with seasoning salt; dry until crisp.	Use as chip for dip. Use within 1 to 2 weeks.
Garlic	Peel cloves and slice in halves or thirds.	Powder dry in blender for seasoning.
Greens	Spinach, chard, etc. Steam until wilted; dry at 110 °F until crisp.	Powder dry in blender for soups.
Herbs	Leave on stems. Dry at 100° to 110° F. Remove from stems. Do not sun-dry.	Store in dark glass, airtight container. Do not crush until ready to use.
Mushrooms	Slice ½-inch thick lengthwise through the stem. Dry at 80° to 90° F for 2 to 3 hours. Increase temperature to 120° F until dry.	Stroganoff, gravy, chicken à la king, scrambled eggs, rice.

Roughing It Easy

DRYING CHART FOR VEGETABLES

Vegetable	Preparation for Drying	Serving Suggestions
Okra	Slice pods ⅜-inch crosswise. Steam 2 to 4 minutes.	"Gumbo soup"; dipped in cornmeal and fried.
Onions	Dice or slice lengthwise. Do not steam.	Chop dry in blender for onion flakes.
Parsnips	Peel and slice ⅜-inch thick. Steam blanch 3 to 4 minutes.	Soups, stews or mashed with butter.
Peas	Shell. Steam blanch 3 to 4 minutes.	Soups, stews.
Peppers	Slice in ⅜-inch slices or dice. Do not steam.	Soups, stews, scrambled eggs.
Potatoes	Peel, slice, steam blanch until translucent. Rinse in cold water.	Hashed browns, soups, stews.
Squash	Slice ⅜-inch thick. Steam blanch 2 to 3 minutes. (Zucchini chips; prepare like cucumber chips.)	Soups, stews, with cheese sauce. Use within 1 to 2 weeks.
Tomatoes	Core and slice ⅜-inch thick. Dry until crisp. Roma tomatoes dry best.	Powder or flake dry in blender. Soups or stews.

Dryness Test

Vegetables should contain less than 5 percent moisture when they are dry; they will feel tough or crisp. Remove vegetables from the dehydrator and allow them to cool to determine the dryness.

Packaging

It is critical that dried vegetables be properly packaged in order to taste good. As with fruits, the ideal choice is vacuum packaging. If you do not own a vacuum packaging device, use freezer bags and place the bags inside plastic or metal containers.

Storage

The storage life for vegetables is shorter than fruits because they are low in acid and sugar. Ideally, they should be used in less than six months when stored at 60° F. Some vegetables such as squash or cucumber should be used within two weeks. As with fruits, temperature is very important. If possible, dried vegetables should be stored in the freezer or refrigerator to maintain the best quality.

Rehydrating Vegetables

When rehydrating vegetables, add just enough water to cover them. The time required may be from 15 minutes to 2 hours, depending on the type of vegetable and the thickness of the slices. Use the leftover water in sauces or soup to retain the most nutrients. Like fresh or frozen vegetables, dried vegetables shouldn't be overcooked.

Many of the vegetables are best served dressed up with a sauce or used in soups or stews. See the chart on vegetables for serving suggestions.

Jerky

Jerky is raw meat that has been sliced thin, seasoned and dried. It is eaten dried and will not reconstitute when water is added. Home-dried jerky is far superior to commercial jerky and usually costs from $6 to $15 per pound compared to $24 to $36 per pound for commercial jerky. Three pounds of lean, fresh meat will make about 1 pound of jerky. Jerky is a popular food for camping and backpacking and is a nutritious snack for everyone.

Types of Meats to Use for Jerky

Any lean meat will make a good jerky, but some cuts are better than others. Rump roasts, sirloin tip roasts, the round and brisket all make excellent jerky. Flank steak is so good that it has earned the reputation of being the "filet mignon" of jerky. Watch the meat specials in the store and try to get the best value.

It's also possible to use less expensive cuts of meat such as chuck roasts, but with the higher fat content, there is less jerky per pound of meat, and the jerky won't keep as long without freezing or refrigeration.

Fully cooked boneless ham may also be made into jerky, but it must be stored in the freezer or refrigerator if you plan to keep it for more than a week or two.

Game meats make delicious jerky, but be sure to keep the meat clean and cold until you're ready to dry it to avoid contamination or spoilage. All game meats should be frozen for sixty days at 0° F (-20° C) as a precaution against disease or parasites.

Preparation for Drying

Cut the meat across the grain in slices about ³⁄₁₆-inch thick. The butcher will frequently cut the meat for you without additional charge. If you slice it yourself, partially freezing the meat makes it easier to slice evenly. Roasts are easier to slice and dry, because there are larger pieces to work with. Then remove the excess fat. Marinate the sliced meat overnight in the refrigerator in a tightly covered container. (See the recipes that follow.) You may also choose to smoke it if you have a meat and fish smoker.

Drying

Jerky should be dried at a temperature of 140° to 160° F to prevent bacterial growth. Temperatures of 120° F or below are unacceptable because they do not kill salmonella or E Coli bacteria.

- Dry the jerky in single layers until a piece cracks but does not break in pieces when you bend it.
- As it dries, blot it with paper towels to remove any excess beads of oil that may collect on the top.
- When it is removed from the dryer, wrap the jerky in paper towels and allow it to stand for 2 to 3 hours to blot the excess fat.
- Cut the jerky into smaller pieces with kitchen scissors and remove any visible fat.
- Store it in a container with a loose-fitting lid for one to two months. For longer storage, place the jerky in an airtight container and freeze.

Marinade Recipes

The following recipes will jerk 2 pounds of sliced lean meat.

SPICY

2 tablespoons water
1 tablespoon A-1 steak sauce
1 tablespoon Worcestershire sauce
2 tablespoons soy sauce
½ teaspoon hickory-flavored liquid smoke

¼ teaspoon pepper
1 teaspoon salt
½ teaspoon onion powder
1 clove crushed garlic

TERIYAKI

½ cup soy sauce
¼ cup brown sugar
1 teaspoon ground ginger

2 cloves crushed garlic
¼ teaspoon pepper

HOT 'N' SPICY

2 tablespoons water	1 teaspoon salt
2 tablespoons Worcestershire sauce	¼ teaspoon cayenne
2 tablespoons A-1 steak sauce	½ teaspoon onion powder
½ teaspoon liquid smoke	2 cloves crushed garlic
¼ teaspoon pepper	

SWEET 'N' SOUR

1 tablespoon soy sauce	¾ teaspoon salt
½ cup vinegar	¼ teaspoon pepper
½ cup pineapple juice	1 teaspoon onion powder
⅓ cup brown sugar	1 clove crushed garlic

Meats for Main Dishes

Home-dehydrated meats do not store well for long periods of time because of the high fat content and also become rancid after several weeks. However, meats may be dried and stored in the freezer until you're ready to take off on a trip and should keep well for a week or so.

Types of Meat to Dry

Lean beef, chicken, turkey, rabbit, fully cooked boneless ham, venison and other lean game meats may all be dried.

Preparation for Drying

Fully cook the meat or poultry and remove any excess fat. It is also possible to use leftover meat that has been cooked to a tender state. Cut the meat into ½-inch cubes, and dry in a dehydrator at 140° to 160° F until crisp.

Storing Meat

Store it in airtight containers or plastic bags in the freezer until you are ready to use the meat.

Reconstituting Dried Meats

Allow the meat to soak in broth or bouillon until it is plump; then cook with other ingredients.

Recipes for the Trail

To help you prepare foods ahead of time for your backpacking trek, or to inspire you to stop and cook a special treat once in a while, here are some suggestions.

HOT COCOA MIX

- Combine

1⅓ cups instant nonfat dry milk

⅓ cup cocoa

2 tablespoons non-dairy creamer (powdered)

½ cup sugar

dash salt

Store in airtight container. For each cup cocoa, add ¼ to ⅓ cup dry mix to 1 cup boiling water.

DRIED APPLE/APRICOT BALLS

- Mix together

1 cup finely chopped dried apricots

1 cup finely chopped dried apples

¼ cup instant nonfat dried milk

- Mix and add to the above

2 tablespoons orange juice concentrate

¾ teaspoon cinnamon

2 tablespoons honey

4 tablespoons light corn syrup

Roll into balls 1 inch in diameter, then roll the balls in powdered sugar. Dry until firm at 140° F.

APRICOT FUDGE

- In a heavy, 2-quart saucepan with buttered sides, combine, heat to boiling and cook to soft-ball stage (238° F) without stirring

1¼ cups granulated sugar

1¼ cups firmly packed light brown sugar

⅓ cup whipping cream

½ cup milk

2 tablespoons butter

- Remove from heat, cool to lukewarm (without stirring) and add

2 teaspoons vanilla

- Beat until candy thickens and loses gloss. Pour into pan after stirring in

⅓ cup finely chopped apricots

⅓ cup finely chopped blanched almonds

Score into squares while still warm. When cool, cut into squares.

APRICOT PEGS

- Thoroughly mix together

1 cup finely chopped dried apricots

1 tablespoon light corn syrup

2 tablespoons honey

1 tablespoon orange juice concentrate

1 teaspoon lemon juice

Knead until mixture clings together, then roll with hands into 4-inch-long "sticks," ¾-inch in diameter.

- Roll in

⅓ cup unsweetened finely grated coconut

Dry in dryer 2 hours at 135° F.

MIXED FRUIT BALLS

- Chop finely in blender or grind in meat grinder

½ cup raisins

1 cup dates

¼ cup dried apricots

½ cup dried prunes

- Add and mix

2 teaspoons lemon juice

1 tablespoon light corn syrup

1 tablespoon orange juice concentrate

¼ cup coconut

4 tablespoons sunflower seeds

- Shape into balls and roll in   ¾ cup finely chopped
                                                  walnuts

Dry in dryer until firm. Wrap individually in plastic wrap.

CRUNCHY GRANOLA BARS

- Stir together and warm in double
  boiler   ½ cup crunchy peanut
                                                  butter
                                                  2 tablespoons honey
                                                  1 teaspoon lemon juice
- Add and mix well   1¼ cups granola with dates

Either roll into balls or press into a lightly greased 8 × 8-inch pan.
Cut into squares after drying until firm in dryer or low oven
(120° F) with door open.

GRANOLA WITH FRUIT

- Mix together   4 cups oats
                                                  1 cup coconut
                                                  ⅓ cup sesame seeds
                                                  1 cup wheat germ
                                                  ½ cup shelled sunflower
                                                  seeds
                                                  ¾ teaspoon cinnamon
                                                  ½ cup rolled wheat
- Mix together and heat   ½ cup honey
                                                  ½ cup light corn syrup
                                                  ½ cup brown sugar
                                                  ½ teaspoon salt
                                                  ⅓ cup orange or apple juice
                                                  concentrate
                                                  ⅓ cup oil
- Add   2 tablespoons vanilla
- Combine all ingredients. Bake at
  200° F until crisp.
- Add   ½ cup raisins or dried
                                                  cherries
                                                  1 cup dried apples, apricots,
                                                  or dates (chopped)
- Bake 10 minutes longer.

BISCUIT MIX

- Stir until well mixed

8 cups sifted all-purpose
    flour

1½ cups nonfat dry milk

2 teaspoons salt

¼ cup baking powder

- Cut in and mix well

1½ cups shortening

Store in a tightly covered container in a cool place. The mix will last several weeks. Makes 10 cups.

BISCUITS

- Add to   2 cups biscuit mix
- from   ⅓ to ½ cup water

Add enough of the water to the dry mix to make a dough that is soft but not sticky. Turn on a lightly floured surface. Roll or pat to ¾-inch thickness. Cut with a biscuit cutter, or cut into squares with a knife. Bake at 450° F for 12 to 15 minutes.

DUMPLINGS

- Mix well

2 cups biscuit mix

⅔ cup water

Drop by spoonfuls onto bubbling stew. Cook 10 minutes uncovered and 10 minutes covered. Place coals on lid of cooking container for best results.

FRUIT DUMPLINGS

- Heat to bubbling

your favorite dried fruit in
    water to cover

- Mix together

2 cups biscuit mix

⅔ cup water

Drop biscuit dough by spoonfuls onto hot fruit. Boil gently 12 minutes without removing cover.

PANCAKE MIX

- Put into a bowl

1 cup biscuit mix

1 egg

½ cup water

Stir just enough to mix. Dip spoonfuls onto a hot griddle. Turn when brown on griddle side and cook until brown on other side. Serve with syrup or preserves.

POTATO PANCAKES

- Mix together

2 cups finely grated raw
  potatoes
¼ cup water
2 eggs, beaten
¼ cup biscuit mix
1¼ teaspoons salt

Form ingredients into patties and drop into ¼-inch hot oil. Turn the potato patties after browning on one side. Brown on the other side and serve.

POTATO-TOMATO SCALLOP

- Combine

2 tablespoons bacon bits
1 5½-ounce box scalloped
  potatoes and sauce mix
2 envelopes instant tomato
  soup
2 cups boiling water
¼ teaspoon oregano leaves

Simmer ingredients slowly until cooked (20 to 30 minutes).

BEEF STEW AND DUMPLINGS

- Place into pot or kettle
- Add and let stand 10 minutes

4 cups boiling water
4 ounces freeze-dried beef
  cubes
4 teaspoons instant minced
  onion

- Add

1 package brown gravy mix
1 package beef-flavored
  mushroom soup mix

- Simmer until thickened.
- Stir in

2 cups (8 ounces each) mixed
  vegetables, drained

Prepare dumplings from biscuit mix; drop by spoonfuls onto the stew and cook for 20 minutes, covered.

CHAPTER 13

Winter Outdoor Adventures

Much of what we've been describing in this book has applied to summer camping, when the weather is fine and there is no problem with being outside after the sun goes down. Winter camping, however, is another story — a lovely one. Many people think camping stops when the snow comes, but you will learn why and how winter can be the best time of year to camp.

Why Camp in the Winter?

According to Jim Phillips, winter camping expert, winter camping provides a number of advantages over summer camping. First of all, there are no bugs! Nor are there snakes, bears, flies or dust. But even if you would trade bugs for freezing temperatures, consider that winter wilderness beauty is breathtaking — an ever-changing scenario of snow, wind and blue sky — and likely to be much less inhabited than summer wilderness. If you like the solitude of the outdoors, winter camping will practically ensure some solitude.

Winter camping also requires a certain fortitude that summer camping does not. Anyone can sleep outside in mild weather. If you like a challenge — if you like knowing that you can survive, and survive *well*, in subfreezing temperatures — then try winter camping. Youth leaders who want to give their kids extra self-confidence have almost no better training ground at their disposal than winter camping. It requires ingenuity and preparedness. With these and some specific skills and equipment, winter camping can be even more comfortable and satisfying than summer camping. You can enjoy the awe of a moonlit night on a snowfield, hike among snow-filled forests or rest in a snowbank (on an insulating pad, of course) as you watch the winter world go about its business.

All you need to change are a few of the things you do in the outdoors. You need to make sensible modifications in the way you think about the relationship between prevention of heat loss, safety, water supply and clothing. This chapter will give you the basics so you can continue to enjoy the outdoors year round.

What It Means to Your Body

Your body consists of the core (the head, neck and trunk), the vital organs, and the extremities (limbs, hands and feet). If the body core temperature drops below 86° F, it can't rewarm itself without external heat and continues to drop until death occurs. Keeping the body core warm is a top priority in winter camping. *Hypothermia* and *frostbite* are two precursors to this extreme lowering of temperature.

Hypothermia

Hypothermia is the lowering of the core body temperature. Three common causes of hypothermia are dehydration, physical exhaustion and wet clothing; a fourth cause is inadequate nutritional intake. Air temperatures do not need to be particularly low for hypothermia to occur—more people die of hypothermia at temperatures between 30° and 50° F than at colder temperatures, largely because they are unprepared and do not pay attention to their bodies' signals.

Dehydration leads to hypothermia because water helps the body metabolize fuel. Less water equals less burning of available fuel; less burning equals less body heat available. Cold air, which is very dry, draws moisture out of your body every time you breathe. It may trick you into believing you're not thirsty when your body really is in need of moisture, so dehydration can be a greater problem in winter than it is in summer. It is imperative that you carry sufficient water *and* take the time to drink it. Don't wait till you're thirsty, and don't just drink enough to slake your thirst. Drink at least a gallon a day while you're outside in the snow.

When you are physically tired or exhausted, body heat production is reduced. Wet clothing also sucks heat out of the body.

Naturally, if you haven't eaten enough to keep your body going, it can't produce sufficient heat. Here are some suggestions to avoid these problems when you are winter camping:

- Stay dry. Put on rain gear before you get wet.
- Beware of the wind, which refrigerates wet clothes.
- Drink more than you think you need.
- Avoid exhaustion by pacing yourself. Allow plenty of time to set up camp and fix meals and be willing to give in to reaching the peak or getting the fish or whatever might drive you past the point of exhaustion. Everything takes longer in cold weather. You must move patiently, with sure motion, rather than hastening beyond what is necessary or healthy.
- Eat food containing complex carbohydrates as well as high-energy dried fruits. Sugary, starchy food only keeps you going for a short time. A high-fat, high-protein recipe that will help keep you warm and your energy level high is the "Iron Man Mix": mix together 1 cup of raisins, 1 cup of nonprocessed cheese (cubed), 1 cup of peanuts and 1 cup of diced beef jerky.

Pay attention to how your body feels. If you begin to shiver, *do something* to warm yourself before numbness and uncontrollable shivering set in. Most hypothermia occurs in wet and windy weather between 30° and 50° F.

Frostbite

Frostbite is the freezing of flesh—most commonly on the extremities and face—caused by exposure to low temperatures, wind chill or direct contact with very cold substances such as metal, subzero gasoline or similar nonfreezing liquids. It is indicated by a whitening or graying of the skin and can be mild or serious, depending on how deep the freezing goes; serious cases can result in amputation. Frostbite can be prevented by all the same prevention measures used for hypothermia, with the addition of the protection of flesh by adequate insulation (see "Winter Camping Clothing" on the next page). If your face or hands begins to show signs of frostbite, warm your hands in your armpits, on your stomach or in your groin, and then warm your facial area with your bare hands.

Water Supply

Some people think that snow is an inexhaustible water supply. Not so. Melting snow in your mouth takes too much energy for the amount of water it returns to your system.

- To have water with you at all times, carry a plastic bottle or flask filled with snow between your underwear and outer clothing. Let your body heat melt the snow as you walk, adding more snow to the container as you drink the liquid. It sounds cold and uncomfortable, but it's easy to get used to and may save you from hypothermia.
- Replenish your water supply from swift-flowing streams that don't freeze. Be sure to purify the water by using water purification filters or chemical treatments, or bringing the water to a rolling boil for 10 or more minutes. Be careful; hang your container from a ski pole or branch rather than leaning over a bank and risk falling in. Remember, wet clothes are a leading cause of hypothermia!
- Melt snow in a pot over a flame. Remember that some snow is wetter than others; if you have a choice, choose ice or slab snow rather than light powder.
- Pack snow into a clean cloth bag and suspend it a yard or so away from an open fire, with a pot underneath to catch the water as it trickles out. On sunny days, sprinkle snow on a large plastic sheet spread out on a slope and position a pot underneath to catch the melting snow.
- Take a filled water bottle to bed with you overnight and it won't freeze. In fact, if you fill it with hot water it can keep you warm. Or bury water bottles or a covered pot under a foot of snow overnight; the snow insulates the water so it's there when you wake for breakfast.

Winter Camping Clothing

Insulation is the key concept in winter camp attire. *Air is our insulating medium* — not the layers of fabric, but the air within and between them. Your body is already warm; what keeps you warm is the air trapped around you, not the coat you are wearing. This is one reason mittens are the hand covering of choice rather than gloves; your fingers keep each other warm. (Always keep your mittens with you by attaching them to a cord that goes around your neck or through the sleeves of your jacket. You wouldn't want to lose one in the cold!)

A Few Words About Layering

Some people think layering is the way to remain warm and pro-tected in outdoor winter activity — long johns, flannel shirt, bibs, jacket, shell, scarf and so on. This is not necessarily so, especially if the fabrics are self-defeating.

Any fabric that absorbs water is less desirable in winter than one that doesn't. Water transfers heat twenty-five times faster than air; you'll stay warm twenty-five times longer if you're dry. It is best to use only synthetic materials; do not mix natural fabrics with snythetics. Cotton absorbs more moisture than any other type of fabric and is acceptable only for outer layers — *not for underwear* — since it takes a long time to dry once it gets wet. Wool is slightly better and warmer than cotton or down because it absorbs water slower, but it still retains moisture and is not the fabric of choice. Synthetics don't absorb or retain water and are preferable to either cotton or wool.

If you layer your clothing, remember the C-O-L-D formula:

- **C — Clean** clothes trap air more effectively than dirty ones.
- **O** — Avoid **overheating** by adjusting your layers according to the outside temperature and your own degree of exertion. Sweating can dampen your clothes and cause chilling later.
- **L — Loose** layers will allow your blood as well as air to circu-late. There is no need to button, zip or tie all your layers tightly around you. This includes footwear. Be sure to use mukluks, booties or overboots cut generously enough to hold your foot and all necessary insulation, and still allow moisture to escape.
- **D — Dry** clothing is a must. Brush snow from your clothes be-fore it melts; loosen clothing to avoid perspiration; don't wear waterproof clothes (since these can hold moisture in), but choose clothes that breathe moisture out.

Insulation

An excellent alternative to standard layering is to use polyure-thane foam in your clothing. It outperforms layering because of how it handles and insulates you, keeping you warm and dry. To adapt your winter clothing, replace the traditional lining with a 1-inch layer of polyurethane foam. (See Figures 13-1, 13-2 and 13-3 on page 226.) All types of winter clothing can be adapted this way, including coats, pants, hats, boots, socks and gloves.

MAKE YOUR OWN BACKPACKING CLOTHING OR EQUIPMENT

If you're clever with a sewing machine and have the time, you may decide to make your own backpacking clothing and/or equipment. It can save you a substantial amount of money. Home-sewn clothing is frequently superior to ready-made, and you can add extras such as sectioned pockets and longer-length jackets for more warmth. A sleeping bag can be made longer, shorter, wider or fuller. A variety of patterns are available and some fabric stores offer kits that include precut pieces and instructions. Outlets in many cities carry backpacking/outdoor fabrics that are quite inexpensive.

Sleeping Gear

A warm and comfortable winter sleeping arrangement is surprisingly easy and inexpensive to construct using a plastic sheet, deicing cloth, moisture-handling pad and foam sleeping bag. Where Arctic explorers used to throw out their sleeping gear because of ice buildup, now you can easily wick the moisture that accumulates in your bag—you can even sleep in wet clothes!—and wake up perfectly dry. Here's how it works:

1. The base is a *plastic sheet*, 12 × 12 feet. Lay it out flat. This is the same 4-mil clear polyethylene you use to rig up your shelter in milder weather.
2. Then spread a *deicing cloth* off to one side of the plastic sheet. The deicing cloth is a piece of uncoated, nonwaterproof nylon fabric, which is 3 × 7 feet. Old parachutes also work well. You can purchase them at Army and Navy stores.
3. Place a *moisture-handling pad* over the deicing cloth. This pad is 1-inch thick and is a low-density, polyurethane foam, also 3 × 7 feet. It moves the moisture away from the sleeping bag and onto the nylon fabric or deicing cloth.

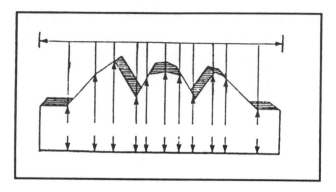

Figure 13-1. Pattern for foam hat

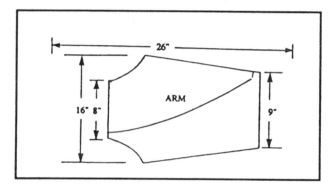

Figure 13-2. Pattern for foam sleeve insert

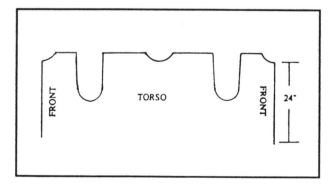

Figure 13-3. Start with a piece of foam 28 inches long and 8 inches wide. Draw the pattern on a piece of stiff paper, cut it out, lay it on the foam and outline it with a felt-tip marker. Use scissors or a very sharp knife to cut the foam around the pattern. Fold until edges meet and glue them together with an adhesive such as 3-M Spray Cement®. Known as "butt-gluing," this method of cementing two flat edges together is used in almost all foam gear construction. Insert the foam lining into your winter clothing. (Used by permission from *Without Fire or Shelter* by Jim Phillips.)

4. Finally, place a *foam sleeping pad* on top of the moisture-handling pad. Or use a sleeping bag that is *not* made from waterproof fabric and insulated with foam. You can insert a foam envelope either inside or outside any bag to create greater warmth.

Since the fabric and foam "breathe," the plastic is needed to block the wind. Fold the narrow length of the plastic over the top of the bag, then fold the remainder over the bag and tuck the extra plastic underneath, burrito style. Finally, fold the end of the plastic under the foot of the bag. As long as it's loose enough to allow you to breathe, it will protect you from the wind and snow. Crawl *all the way in*, covering your entire head — including your nose and mouth — and pulling the drawstring of your bag closed. You won't suffocate because *all the fabric and foam in this system breathes*, so you will be perfectly safe.

The warmth from your body will drive moisture through your clothes and the sleeping bag until it hits the plastic or nylon and freezes. In the morning, you'll be warm and dry. Shake the ice off the plastic and deicing cloth, and you'll be ready to pack up and move on. Or, if you're staying put, spread your sleeping gear out to dry; however, this system keeps you warm even if the foam becomes wet.

Snow is more shapeable than dirt and you can actually have a delightfully comfortable contoured sleeping place if you sculpture the snow where you sleep. This also goes for lounging or sitting — simply sculpture the snow, insert foam or cardboard (or even plastic with a pillow inside) between the snow and your bottom, and you have a comfortable place to pass the winter hours. Voilá!

Winter Backpacking Necessities

Hauling your gear is tricky only because much of your equipment is bulky since it's needed for added insulation. Try an external frame pack or even a toboggan to make the hiking easier.

Fire is not a requirement for winter camping; if you correctly dress, eat and build a shelter/sleeping system, you can do very well without a fire. Nevertheless, it's important to know how to make a fire (see chapter five) and to carry matches and a small stove if that's your choice.

Snow Domes

It's perfectly fine to use a tent as shelter against the wind and snow when you're winter camping, but an even better shelter is one made of snow itself. Snow is a good insulator, and as William O. Douglas says, "One has to lie deep in the snow to learn how warm and protective it is. A den in the snow confines the body heat like a blanket or overcoat. It is a snug place, no matter how the wind may howl. One who holes up in the snow understands better the mysteries of the woods in the winter. He knows why the severe weather grouse squirm their way under soft snow and be quiet. He understands why deer bury themselves in drifts, lying a half-day or more with just their heads sticking out. He learns something about the comfort of the bear in hibernation." (Quoted from *The Boy Scout Fieldbook*, 3rd Edition, page 330, Irving, Texas, 1984.)

To build a snow dome (Figure 13-4), you'll need thirty 10-inch sticks or dowels painted black on one end, a sturdy shovel and some patience. Begin making the snow dome by shoveling a mound of snow about 6 feet high and 10 to 12 feet in diameter at the base. If you're at home and have a snow blower, this can be done very quickly. Simply start walking in a large circle, gradually blowing all the snow to the center. Once the snow is all piled up, push all the sticks (painted end first) into it at about 18-inch intervals, pointing toward the center. Let the mound set for at least 2 hours, though overnight would be better. This will allow the snow to settle and consolidate.

Using your shovel, cut a 2-foot-high entrance to the mound as close to the ground as possible. Start hollowing out the mound, piling the snow at the side of the entrance as a wind barrier. Continue digging until you see the ends of the sticks. You should now have a roomy, peaceful shelter.

A second type of shelter you can build is the snow cave. It uses the same principles as the snow dome, except that it is built in deep drifts or steep, stable snow slopes. If you decide to build this type, however, please be aware of extreme avalanche danger. Begin by digging a tunnel in the drift, angling it upward several

Figure 13-4. Snow dome

feet. Excavate a dome-shaped room at the top of the tunnel following the same techniques as for the snow dome, using sticks pushed into the drift to indicate the thickness. Smooth the curved roof to remove sharp edges that may cause moisture to drip on you. Before you sleep in your snow dome or cave, follow these safety precautions:

1. Punch out a few holes at a 45° angle to the floor with a ski pole or long stick for ventilation. Occasionally check to make sure these holes are still open and that drifting or blowing snow has not blocked them.
2. Never burn a stove or lantern inside as many give off poisonous carbon monoxide gas. Also, they use up available oxygen. Do all of your cooking outside.
3. You may use candles inside your shelter for light and warmth.

Helpful Hints

1. Wear appropriate, waterproof clothing. As much as possible, keep the snow brushed off your clothing. Colorful outer clothing will make you more visible in case of an emergency.
2. To avoid losing equipment in the snow, keep everything stored on your sled or in your pack or pockets. You could even tie brightly colored ribbon to small pieces of gear so it can be easily seen.
3. As much as possible, keep the entrance to your snow shelter

lower than the floor (rising warm air won't escape through it and heavier cold air can't come in). It can be as much as 30° warmer inside a snow shelter than outside.

4. Be sure to have a plastic ground cloth or mat to sit on so you will stay dry.

Fun Winter Activities

A Winter Picnic

You probably know the kind of appetite you can build up when sledding, skating, skiing or playing outside in the snow, so a winter picnic may be a good idea! Be sure you take along a poncho to lay over the snow. Cardboard boxes for sitting can later be used for sledding.

Hot Box or Fireless Cooker

For your winter picnic, you need to keep the hot food in a hot box. Choose a box 3 to 4 inches larger than your food container. Place a 1-inch stack of newspapers on the bottom of the box. Line each side of the box with an additional 1-inch-thick pad of newspapers. Make sure the food and its container are very hot! A thick aluminum pot or heavy cast-iron kettle with a good lid will help the food retain heat the best. Place the container of hot food in the newspaper-lined box. If the newspapers do not fit snugly around the container, stuff in additional newspapers so the container nests tightly and can't move. Place at least 1 inch of newspapers over the top of the container, then close the box tightly over the newspaper. This insulated box will help keep food hot for at least 3 hours.

Chili in Bread Bowls

Heat your favorite chili until very hot. Bake or buy 3- to 4-inch hard rolls. Slice off the top quarter of each roll. Carefully hollow out the center of each roll, leaving a ½-inch crust to form each bowl. Place in an airtight container or plastic bag. When you are ready to serve, spoon chili into the edible bowls. Stew and thick hearty soups also taste delicious served in bread bowls.

Chili Dog on a Bun

Tie a 12-inch length of dental floss around a hot dog and heat the hot dog in a saucepan with chili. Lower the hot dog into a thermos, leaving the string hanging out of the top. Pour the chili around the hot dog and then cap the thermos. Use the end of the floss to pull the hot dog out of the thermos and into a hot dog bun. Pull the floss through the hot dog and spoon the chili onto the bun for a delicious chili dog.

Hot Chili Chips in a Bag

For this chili idea, you'll need either individual bags of corn chips or corn chips in a heavy-duty, self-sealing plastic bag. Open the bag and pour hot chili from a thermos over the chips. Use a plastic spoon to enjoy these chili chips in a bag.

Snowman in Hot Chocolate

Turn two large marshmallows into a snowman to float on your hot chocolate. For each snowman, dip the tip of a toothpick in blue food coloring. Use it to dot eyes and a nose on one marshmallow, and a vertical row of buttons on a second. Use another toothpick dipped in red food coloring to paint the mouth of the snowman. Pack the marshmallows in self-sealing bags or airtight plastic containers. Heat chocolate drink, then pour into thermos. To serve, pour hot chocolate in a cup, then float the two marshmallows together on the hot drink to form your snowman.

Ice Fishing

Before you do any ice fishing, be sure to obtain a fishing license. When you purchase it, ask for information on places to go as well as rules and regulations. Remember, regulations vary from state to state and season to season.

You will need proper clothing. You'll also need waterproof boots (preferably insulated ones), several pairs of warm socks (you can purchase battery-powered warming socks at most camping stores), and at least two pairs of gloves (they're sure to get wet).

You'll also need proper equipment. This includes an ax or ice auger to make the hole; a large scoop or strainer to remove ice chips from the hole; a fishing pole — a regular pole will work, but there are ones made especially for ice fishing; hooks, #2 up to #14, single or treble; weights, small lead weight sinkers; lures, any type; bait, salmon eggs, angle worms or plastic worms; a knife for cleaning the fish; and something to sit on. You could get by with a bucket turned upside down, but it would be better to take along a lawn chair and thick quilt or sleeping bag for padding and warmth. Also, take a small hibachi grill or portable propane grill to provide warmth as well as a place to keep coffee or hot chocolate warm. Finally, it's a good idea to set up a regular camping tent for protection from the weather. When you have all of your equipment together, tie it to a sled for easy transportation across snow and ice.

When you reach your destination, it is very easy to find out if the ice is thick enough. Simply ask people at the lake or other ice fishers in the area. If there isn't anyone to ask, drill a test hole. The ice should be a minimum of 6 inches deep. Drill a hole and enjoy the catch. Do *not* attempt ice fishing on rivers; it can be very dangerous and is not for beginners.

A Final Word

Winter camping and other outdoor activities require as much if not more creativity as camping during the other seasons. Common sense and safety awareness make winter camping an excellent alternative to staying around the house. For more information on winter camping, see *The Boy Scout Handbook* (10th Edition, 1992) and Clair Rees's *Backpacking* (7th Edition, Winchester Press). May many happy Decembers, Januarys and Februarys include your camping pleasure!

Conclusion

One of the reasons I love camping is the feeling I get when I solve a problem creatively. And I believe that once you discover and enjoy that feeling for yourself, you'll be hooked, too. Camping allows you to create many memories for you and your family, and if I have somehow led your way in the discovery of self-sustenance and family memories, I will have accomplished my goals for *Roughing It Easy*.

Notes

Recipe Index

Notes

Roughing It Easy

Index

NESTING, *COCOONING,* BURROWING...

That is what America is doing in the '90s ... and Dian Thomas shows how to make it easy and fun!

Americans are finding their greatest pleasures at home. Enjoying their families. Entertaining their friends. And they're looking for ways to do it easily and inexpensively. Now you can get in on the excitement. Choose from Dian's complete assortment of books and videos.

Let the fun begin!

Holiday Fun

Dian Thomas is back, with a year's worth ... many years' worth ... of fun for readers. In **Holiday Fun**, she treats you to exciting ideas that turn mere holiday observances into opportunities to exercise your imagination and turn the festivity all the way up!! **Holiday Fun** gives you a year-round collection of festive ideas and recipes to make every holiday special. You'll discover interesting tidbits of information about many holidays, why we observe them, and how to celebrate them with fun. You'll discover ideas for:

- A super Super Bowl party
- Silly April Fool's Day pranks
- An exciting egg hunt for Easter
- Homemade gifts for Mother's Day and Father's Day
- Labor Day recipes and ideas for a family get-together
- Eerie decorations, creative costumes, and spooky treats for Halloween
- Creative Christmas ideas ...

... and more. From New Year's to Christmas.

Holiday Fun is loaded with creative and fun tips, recipes, and decorations. Dian's ideas are winners!! 176 pages, full-color photos. **$19.99.**

ORDER TOLL FREE: 1-800-846-6355

FUN AT HOME WITH DIAN THOMAS

This collection of creative ideas, demonstrated on ABC's *Home* show, has something for everyone. Dian shows you how to keep the kids busy on a rainy day, make Kick-the-Can Ice Cream, and craft unique holiday decorations. It's a treasure of fun do-it-yourself or with-your-children projects! 200 pages with over 500 illustrations. **$14.95.**

TODAY'S TIPS FOR EASY LIVING

From her appearances on the *Today* show, Dian shares over 400 great ideas for today's time-strapped families. She has tips for quick meals, stay-at-home vacations, homemade toys, rainy-day activities, kids' costumes, and more. 160 pages with 265 color photos. **$12.95.**

ROUGHING IT EASY

Even the camp cooks have fun when they're **Roughing It Easy!** This *New York Times* best-seller is chock-full of recipes and great ideas that make outdoor camping and cooking an adventure. It is the complete camper's bible. Cook eggs and bacon in a paper bag, boil water in a paper cup, and start a fire with steel wool and batteries! There are suggestions for equipment selection, fire building, campfire cooking, and even drying your own foods for backpacking! If you love the out-of-doors, **Roughing It Easy** is for you. 240 pages. **$14.99.**

DUTCH OVEN COOKING BASICS

TV personality Dian Thomas, an avid Dutch oven cook, is your guide to learning everything you need to know about getting started with Dutch oven cooking. She walks you step-by-step through the process as she energetically prepares delicious recipes and shows unique ways to use your oven.

Filmed in Utah, the heart of Dutch oven country, this video gets down to the very basics of Dutch oven cooking. Helpful tips take the viewer through oven selection, seasoning, cleaning, and storing. 30 minutes. **$9.95.**

VIDEOS

• **Let's Party!** • **Quick & Easy Holiday Ideas** • **Creating Fun & Easy Toy Projects**

Each video gives you step-by-step instructions and patterns for unforgettable party ideas, holiday decorations, and fun toys! 30 minutes. **$9.95** each.

ORDER BY MAIL OR CALL TOLL FREE 1-800-846-6355

Send with payment or credit card information to:
The Dian Thomas Company, PO Box 171107, Holladay, UT 84117
or **call TOLL FREE 1-800-846-6355.**

Name _____

Address _____

City/State/ZIP_____

Telephone (   ) _____

☐   Check/Money Order (please, no currency)
    Make checks payable to: **The Dian Thomas Co.**

☐   Visa   ☐   MasterCard   ☐   Discover

Signature_____ Exp. Date_____

Card Number_____
                        (Please list all numbers on card)

DESCRIPTION	QTY	UNIT PRICE	TOTAL
Holiday Fun		19.99	
Roughing It Easy		14.99	
Fun at Home		14.95	
Today's Tips for Easy Living		12.95	
Dutch Oven Cooking Basics video		9.95	
Let's Party! video		9.95	
Quick & Easy Holiday Ideas video		9.95	
Creating Fun & Easy Toy Projects video		9.95	

*Add $3.00 shipping/handling for first item and
$1.00 for each additional item.

                                   Subtotal $_____

               Shipping and handling* $_____

       Utah residents add 6.25% sales tax $_____

• Canadian residents add 30% to total.   **TOTAL** $_____